Createspace Publishing

4900 Lacross Rd,
North Charleston, SC 29406

www.createspace.com

GEOMETRY
for
SAT & ACT
with
55 Practice Tests

Published by Createspace: October 08, 2018

ISBN 13: 978-1544853765
ISBN 10: 1544853769

Tayyip Oral, MBA
Veysel Karatas, M. Ed.

GEOMETRY
for
SAT & ACT
with
55 Practice Tests

www.555mathbooks.com

555 Math Book series

1) 1000 Logic & Reasoning Questions for Gifted and Talented Elementary School Students
2) 555 SAT Math (555 Questions with Solution)
3) 555 GEOMETRY (555 Questions with Solution)
4) 555 GEOMETRY Problems for High School Students
5) 555 ACT Math (555 Questions with Solution)
6) 555 ACT Math (555 Questions with Answers)
7) 555 ADVANCED Math Problems - for Middle School Students
8) 555 MATH IQ Questions for High School Students
9) 555 MATH IQ Questions for Middle School Students
10) 555 MATH IQ Questions for Elementary School Students
11) 555 GEOMETRY Formula handbook for SAT, ACT, GRE
12) GEOMETRY Formula Handbook
13) ALGEBRA Handbook for Middle School Students
14) GEOMETRY for SAT&ACT (555 Questions with Answers)
15) 555 Gifted and Talented for Middle School Students
16) ALGEBRA for the New SAT (1111 Questions with Answers)
17) ALGEBRA for the ACT (1080 Questions with Answers)
18) 555 MATH IQ for Elementary School Students (2nd Edition)
19) TSI MATH (Texas Success Initiative)
20) ACCUPLACER MATH PREP

Order the 555 Math Book series

www.555academy.com

www.amazon.com

and

www.barnesandnoble.com

www.555mathbooks.com

Table of Contents

Preface

Geometry for SAT and ACT with 55 Practice Test book provides excellent Geometry practice tests. It is an excellent book for high school students to improve their Geometry skills by focusing on points, lines, rays, angles, triangles, polygons, circles, perimeter, area, and more.

Additionally, the material in this book includes Geometry questions with their answers. Also, this book helps students and teachers with the ACT and SAT preparations. Readers find a comprehensive review of the essential Geometry topics taught in high school specifically.

Also, the Geometry practice tests presented in this book based upon the most recent state-level tests and include almost every type of geometry question that one can expect to find on high school level standardized tests.

The Authors

TEST 1
(Angles)

1) BD bisects angle ABC. What is the value of x?

A) 10
B) 12
C) 15
D) 18
E) 20

2) What is the measurement of angle EBC?

A) 40
B) 50
C) 60
D) 70
E) 80

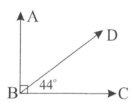

3) If the measure of angle DBC is 44^0, what is the measure of angle ABD?

A) 44
B) 45
C) 46
D) 47
E) 48

4) If the measure of angle ABD is $(x+10)^0$, what is the measure of angle DBC?

A) 40
B) 42
C) 43
D) 44
E) 50

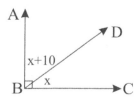

5) If the ratio of the measure of angle ABD and the measure of angle DBC is two-thirds what is the measure of angle DBC?

A) 62°
B) 68°
C) 70°
D) 72°
E) 54°

6) d_1 and d_2 are the parallel. What is the value of the x?

A) 46
B) 47
C) 48.3
D) 49
E) 50

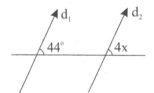

7) d_1 and d_2 are the parallel. What is the value of the x?

A) 10
B) 11
C) 12
D) 13
E) 14

8) d_1 and d_2 are the parallel. What is the value of the x?

A) 10
B) 20
C) 30
D) 40
E) 50

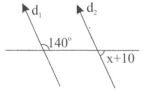

9) d_1 and d_2 are the parallel. What is the value of the x?

A) 18
B) 20
C) 22
D) 24
E) 26

10) What is the value of the x?

A) 20
B) 22
C) 24
D) 25
E) 30

11) If the different measure of angle ABD and measure of angle DBC is 26⁰, what is the measure of angle ABD?

A) 100
B) 103
C) 106
D) 110
E) 120

12) If the ratio of the measure of angle ABD and the measure of angle DBC is 3, what is the measure of angle DBC?

A) 40
B) 41
C) 42
D) 43
E) 45

13) What is the value of y–x?

A) 50
B) 54
C) 48
D) 60
E) 62

14) The measure of angle A and the measure of angle B are the complementary angles. The measure of angle A is $(3x+3)^0$, and the measure of angle B is $(2x+2)^0$. What is the measure of angle B?

A) 28   B) 30   C) 32
D) 36   E) 38

15) d_1 and d_2 are the parallel. What is the value of the x?

A) 10
B) 20
C) 25
D) 30
E) 35

TEST 2
(Angles)

1) d_1 and d_2 are the parallel. What is the value of the x?

A) 10
B) 11
C) 12
D) 13
E) 14

2) What is the value of the x?

A) 20
B) 25
C) 30
D) 35
E) 40

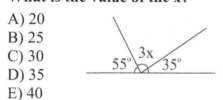

3) d_1 and d_2 are the parallel. What is the value of the x?

A) 20
B) 25
C) 28
D) 30
E) 32

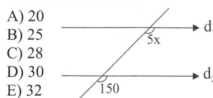

4) The measure of angle ABC is 90^0. What is the measure of angle BAC?

A) 40
B) 45
C) 50
D) 55
E) 60

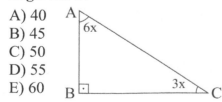

5) The measure of angle BCA is 23^0, what is the measure of angle CAB?

A) 67
B) 64
C) 63
D) 60
E) 58

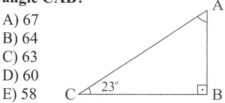

6) If the different measure of angle ABD and measure of angle DBC is 20^0, what is the measure of angle DBC?

A) 20
B) 25
C) 30
D) 35
E) 40

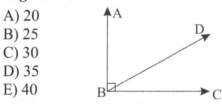

7) If the ratio of the measure of angle ABD and the measure of angle DBC is 4, what is the measure of angle ABD?

A) 62
B) 66
C) 68
D) 70
E) 72

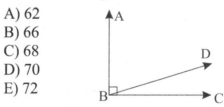

8) If the different measure of angle ABD and measure of angle DBC is 30^0, what is the measure of angle ABD?

A) 100   B) 105
C) 110   D) 115
E) 120

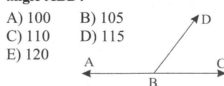

9) What is the measure of angle DBC?

A) 33
B) 43
C) 53
D) 63
E) 73

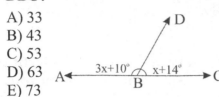

10) d_1 and d_2 are the parallel. What is the value of the x?

A) 20
B) 25
C) 30
D) 33
E) 36

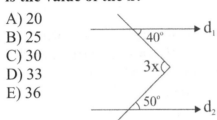

11) What is the measure of angle 2x?

A) 180-3y
B) 180+3y
C) 110+3y
D) 110-3y
E) 110+2y

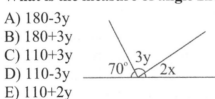

12) What is the measure of angle $\dfrac{3x}{2}$?

A) 90-4y
B) 90+4y
C) 100-4y
D) 45+2y
E) 45-2y

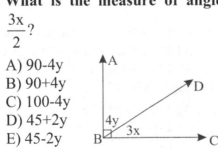

13) d_1 and d_2 are the parallel. What is the value of the 4y?

A) 11
B) 22
C) 66
D) 88
E) 100

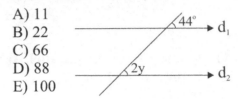

14) What is the measure of angle 3y?

A) 90+2x
B) 90+3x
C) 180+6y
D) 90-2x
E) 90-4x

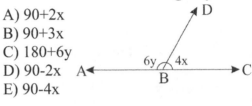

15) What is the measure of angle $\dfrac{3y}{2}$?

A) 360–27–y
B) 180–27–y
C) 160+27+y
D) 360+47+2x
E) 156.5–x

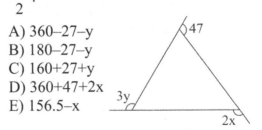

TEST 3
(Slope, Parallel line, and Perpendicular line)

1) What is the slope of the line that passes through the points (4, 9) and (7, 11)?

A) $\dfrac{4}{3}$ B) $\dfrac{3}{4}$ C) $\dfrac{2}{3}$

D) 2 E) 1

2) What is the slope of the line that passes through the points (8, 6) and (–2, 10)?

A) $-\dfrac{2}{5}$ B) $\dfrac{2}{5}$ C) $\dfrac{5}{2}$

D) $-\dfrac{5}{2}$ E) 2

3) What is the slope of the line that passes through the points $\left(2\sqrt{2},\ 2\sqrt{3}\right)$ and $\left(3\sqrt{2}, 2\sqrt{27}\right)$?

A) $\sqrt{2}$ B) $\sqrt{3}$ C) $2\sqrt{2}$

D) $2\sqrt{6}$ E) $\dfrac{4\sqrt{3}}{\sqrt{2}}$

4) What is the slope of the line that passes through the points (14, 12) and (10, 10)?

A) 1 B) $\dfrac{1}{2}$ C) $-\dfrac{1}{2}$

D) –1 E) –2

5) What is the equation of the line through the point (6, 8) that has a slope of 5?

A) y=5x+14 B) y=14x+6

C) y=6x–23 D) y=3x+7

E) y=5x–22

6) What is the equation of the line through the point (7, 3) that has a slope of 6?

A) y=6x–16 B) y=6x–14

C) y=6x–39 D) y=5x–26

E) y=6x–12

7) Line m_1 has the equation y=–3x+8. Line m_2 is parallel to m_1 and passes through the point (3, 7). What is the equation of m_2?

A) y= –3x+16 B) y= –3x+15

C) y=2x+8 D) y= –2x+13

E) y=8x+10

8) Line m_1 has the equation $y = \sqrt{2} + 2x$. Line m_2 is parallel to m_1 and passes through the point (6, 9). What is the equation of m_2?

A) $y = \sqrt{3}x + 2\sqrt{3} - 1$ B) y=7-2x

C) $y = \sqrt{3}x + 2\sqrt{3}$ D) y=2x-3

E) $y = -\sqrt{3}x + 2\sqrt{3} - 1$

9) y=9+19x. What is the slope of the question?

A) −9   B) 9   C) 19

D) −19   E) 1

13) m_1 equation line: y=7x+5;
m_2 equation line: y=ax+13;
m_1 is perpendicular of m_2 line.
What is the value of a?

A) 7   B) −7   C) $\dfrac{1}{7}$

D) $\dfrac{3}{13}$ E) $-\dfrac{1}{7}$

10) 7x+9y+22=0. What is the slope of the question?

A) 7   B) $-\dfrac{7}{9}$ C) 9

D) $-\dfrac{3}{8}$ E) $-\dfrac{8}{3}$

14) What is the equation of the line with Slope=9, y-intercept =8?

A) y=9x+8   B) y= −9x+6

C) y=5x+7   D) y=8x+9

E) y= −8x−9

11) $y = \sqrt{13}x + 7\sqrt{11}$. What is the slope of the question?

A) $-\sqrt{13}$ B) $\sqrt{11}$ C) $-3\sqrt{3}$

D) $\sqrt{13}$ E) $\dfrac{1}{\sqrt{3}}$

15) m_1 line: $y = \dfrac{7x}{4} + 6$.

m_2 line: $y = \dfrac{3x}{7} + 9$.

What is the sum of slopes?

A) $\dfrac{51}{37}$ B) $\dfrac{71}{43}$ C) $\dfrac{19}{15}$

D) $-\dfrac{19}{15}$ E) $\dfrac{61}{28}$

12) Line m_1 has equation y=-3x+6
What is the equation of line m_2 that passes through B(5, −3) and is perpendicular to m_1.

A) $y = \dfrac{2x}{3} + \dfrac{2}{3}$ B) $y = -\dfrac{2x}{3} - \dfrac{2}{3}$

C) $y = \dfrac{x}{3} + \dfrac{4}{3}$ D) $y = \dfrac{x}{3} - \dfrac{14}{3}$

E) $y = \dfrac{-x}{3} - 1$

TEST 4
(Slope)

1) $y=5x+4$. What is the slope of the question?

   A) -4 B) 4   C) 12

   D) $\dfrac{4}{5}$ E) 5

2) $5x+11y+22=0$. What is the slope of the question?

   A) $\dfrac{5}{11}$ B) $-\dfrac{5}{11}$ C) 5

   D) -11 E) $\dfrac{11}{5}$

3) $y = \sqrt{2}x + 3\sqrt{3}$. What is the slope of the question?

   A) $\sqrt{2}$ B) $-\sqrt{3}$ C) $3\sqrt{3}$

   D) $-3\sqrt{3}$ E) $-\dfrac{1}{\sqrt{3}}$

4) $y = \sqrt{6}x + 8$. What is the slope of the question?

   A) $\dfrac{\sqrt{2}}{\sqrt{3}}$ B) $\dfrac{\sqrt{3}}{\sqrt{2}}$ C) $\dfrac{-\sqrt{2}}{\sqrt{3}}$

   D) $\sqrt{6}$ E) $\sqrt{3}$

5) Line m has equation $y=7x+12$. Which equation is parallel to line m?

   A) $y=-7x+12$ B) $y=3x+7$

   C) $y=7x+4$ D) $y=-12x+7$

   E) $y=4x+4$

6) m_1 line: $8x+3y+9=0$;
m_2 line: $ax+7y+11=0$;
if m_1 and m_2 are parallel, what is the value of a?

   A) $\dfrac{56}{3}$ B) $-\dfrac{56}{3}$ C) $\dfrac{8}{7}$

   D) $\dfrac{7}{8}$ E) 6

7) m_1 line: $9x+11y=14$;
m_2 line: $ax+6y=15$;
m_1 line is perpendicular m_2, what is the value of a?

   A) $-\dfrac{22}{3}$ B) $\dfrac{3}{22}$ C) $-\dfrac{11}{3}$

   D) $\dfrac{7}{11}$ E) $\dfrac{11}{6}$

8) What is the equation of line d_1?

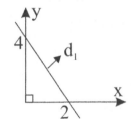

   A) $\dfrac{x}{4}+\dfrac{y}{2}=1$ B) $\dfrac{x}{2}+\dfrac{y}{4}=-1$

   C) $\dfrac{x}{2}+\dfrac{y}{4}=1$ D) $\dfrac{x}{2}+\dfrac{y}{4}=4$

   E) $2x+4y=4$

9) What is the equation of line d_1?

A) $\dfrac{x}{7} - \dfrac{y}{7} = 1$

B) $\dfrac{x}{7} + \dfrac{y}{7} = 14$

C) $7x + 7y = 14$

D) $x + y = 14$

E) $x + y = 7$

10) A(7, 5) and B(11, 15), What is the slope of $\overrightarrow{AB}$?

A) $\dfrac{1}{3}$ B) $\dfrac{1}{2}$ C) $\dfrac{3}{4}$

D) $\dfrac{5}{2}$ E) $\dfrac{3}{2}$

11) A(9, 5) and B(6, 7). What is the slope of $\overrightarrow{AB}$?

A) $\dfrac{5}{3}$ B) $\dfrac{5}{4}$ C) $-\dfrac{2}{3}$

D) $\dfrac{1}{3}$ E) $\dfrac{1}{4}$

12) $A\left(\dfrac{1}{3}, \dfrac{1}{7}\right)$, $B\left(\dfrac{1}{2}, \dfrac{1}{2}\right)$, What is the slope of $\overrightarrow{AB}$?

A) $\dfrac{14}{15}$ B) $\dfrac{15}{7}$ C) $-\dfrac{13}{12}$

D) $\dfrac{12}{13}$ E) 2

13) $\dfrac{8x}{9} + \dfrac{5y}{7} + 9 = 0$. What is the slope of the question?

A) $\dfrac{8}{9}$ B) $\dfrac{9}{8}$ C) $-\dfrac{56}{45}$

D) $-\dfrac{9}{4}$ E) $-\dfrac{7}{9}$

14) What is the equation of line d_1?

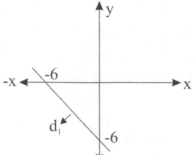

A) $x + y = 6$ B) $x + y = -6$

C) $y = x - 6$ D) $y = -x + 12$

E) $2x + y = 6$

15) What is the equation of line d_1?

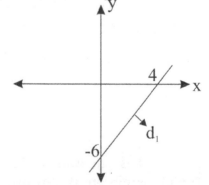

A) $\dfrac{x}{4} + \dfrac{y}{6} = 1$ B) $\dfrac{x}{6} + \dfrac{y}{4} = 1$

C) $\dfrac{x}{4} - \dfrac{y}{6} = 1$ D) $\dfrac{x}{4} - \dfrac{y}{6} = -1$

E) $4x + 6y = 24$

TEST 5
(Triangles and Angles)

1) If the measure of angle BAC is 68⁰, what is the measure of angle ABC?

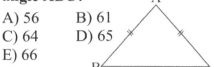

A) 56   B) 61
C) 64   D) 65
E) 66

2) The measure of angle BAC is 66⁰, and the measure of angle ACD is 116⁰, what is the measure of angle ABC?

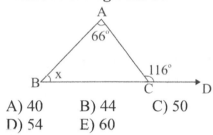

A) 40   B) 44   C) 50
D) 54   E) 60

3) The measure of angle BAC is 50⁰, and the measure of angle ACD is (4x)⁰, what is the value of x?

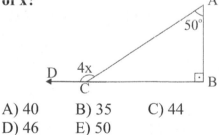

A) 40   B) 35   C) 44
D) 46   E) 50

4) The measure of angle BAC is (6x)⁰ and the measure of angle ACB is (4x)⁰, what is the value of 3x?

A) 60   B) 30
C) 27   D) 72
E) 80

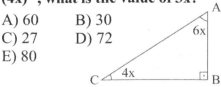

5) ∠B=90⁰, ∠A=∠C=3x, What is the measure of angle BAC?

A) 25
B) 20
C) 18
D) 16
E) 45

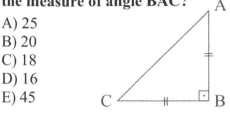

6) The measure of angle BAC is 134⁰ and AB=AC, What is the measure of angle ABC?

A) 30
B) 29
C) 28
D) 23
E) 26

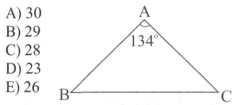

7) ∠A=72°, ∠B=68°, ∠C=50°. Order the lengths of the sides of ABC from greatest to least?

A) AB>BC>AC
B) BC>AC>AB
C) AC>AB>BC
D) BA>BC>AC
E) AB=AC>BC

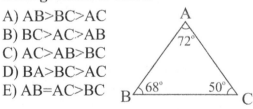

8) What is the measure of angle x?

A) 108
B) 109
C) 110
D) 120
E) 121

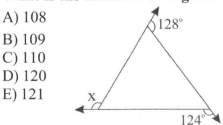

9) What is the measure of angle 2x+6y?

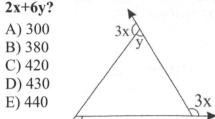

A) 300
B) 380
C) 420
D) 430
E) 440

10) What is the measure of angle α?

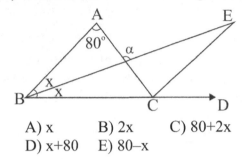

A) x   B) 2x   C) 80+2x
D) x+80   E) 80−x

11) BD=DC=AD, ∠C=3x, ∠B=y, what is the value of 2y+6x?

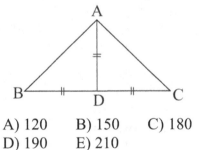

A) 120   B) 150   C) 180
D) 190   E) 210

12) AB=AC, AD=DC, What is the value of 2x?

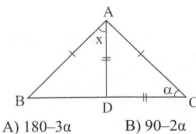

A) 180−3α   B) 90−2α
C) 180−3α   D) 180−4α
E) 360−6α

13) ∠ADC=90°, ∠C=90°, ∠DAC=66°, ∠E=α=?

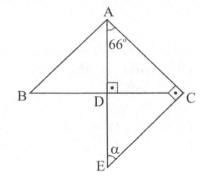

A) 24   B) 26   C) 28
D) 30   E) 32

14) AB=AC, BD=BC, what is the value of 6a?

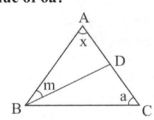

A) 180+m   B) 180−m
C) 360+m   D) 360+2m
E) 540-3x

15) AB=BC=AC, AC=DC, ∠D=2x, what is the value of x^2?

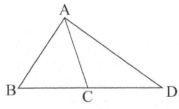

A) 144   B) 225   C) 169
D) 289   E) 400

TEST 6

(Congruence and Triangles)

Use the following information and figure for questions 1-2.

$\angle A=25^{o}$, $\angle F=(4y–3)^{o}$, and $ABC \cong FED$

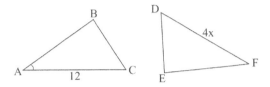

1) **What is the value of x?**

   A) 1   B) 2   C) 3
   D) 4   E) 5

2) **What is the value of y?**

   A) 8   B) 7   C) 6
   D) 5   E) 4

Use the following information and figure for questions 3-4.

$AE=14$, $\angle D=44^{o}$, $FL=3x+3$, and $\angle K=(5y–8)^{o}$, $BCDE \cong FGHKL$

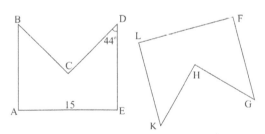

3) **What is the value of x?**

   A) 6   B) 5   C) 4
   D) 3   E) 2

4) **What is the value of 5y?**

   A) 45   B) 44   C) 52
   D) 51   E) 50

5) $\angle A=\angle E$, what is the value of x?

   A) 66
   B) 64
   C) 60
   D) 50
   E) 33

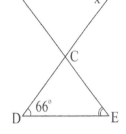

6) $\angle F=63^{o}$, $\angle C=(3x+3)^{o}$, what is the value of x?

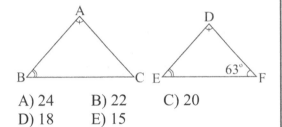

   A) 24   B) 22   C) 20
   D) 18   E) 15

7) $\angle B=\angle D=56^{o}$, $\angle E=(3x+15)$, $\angle C=\angle F=64^{o}$, what is the value of x?

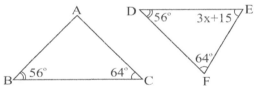

   A) 15   B) 16   C) 17
   D) 18   E) 20

8) $\angle ABC \cong EDF$, $\angle B=108^{o}$, $\angle A=42^{o}$, $\angle F=4x–4$, what is the value of 2x?

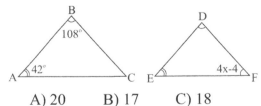

   A) 20   B) 17   C) 18
   D) 16   E) 15

9) ABC is the equilateral triangle. What is the value of 2y-x?

A) 90
B) 120
C) 160
D) 180
E) 220

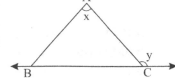

10) ABC is the isosceles triangle, $\angle A = 5x$, $\angle B = 3x - 20^o$, what is the value of x?

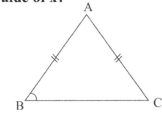

A) 10   B) 25   C) 40
D) 55   E) 70

11) ABC is the isosceles triangle, $\angle A = 2x$, $\angle B = 2x + 40^o$, what is the value of x?

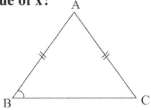

A) $\frac{130}{3}$ B) $\frac{130}{7}$ C) $\frac{140}{5}$

D) $\frac{140}{3}$ E) $\frac{50}{3}$

12) What is the sum the perimeter of all triangles?

A) 70
B) 64
C) 60
D) 50
E) 52

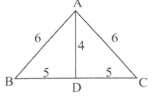

13) ABC, DCE, and FEK are the equilateral triangles. BK=18cm. What is the sum of all triangle perimeters?

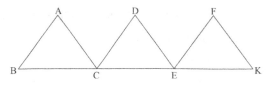

A) 54   B) 56   C) 58
D) 60   E) 66

14) ABC is the right triangle and AB=BC, $\angle B = 90^o$, DEF is the equilateral triangle. What is the value of $\angle 2F + \angle C$?

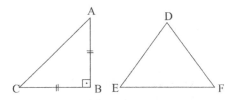

A) 200   B) 180   C) 165
D) 170   E) 122

15) ABC is the equilateral triangle. $\angle BAC = 22^o$, what is the value of $\angle CAD$?

A) 35
B) 38
C) 39
D) 40
E) 44

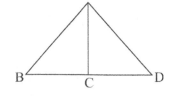

TEST 8

(Bisectors and median of a triangle)

1) If $\angle ABD$ is bisected by ray $\overrightarrow{BD}$. $\angle B = 90^\circ$. What is the value of x?

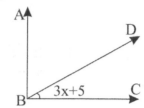

A) $\dfrac{20}{3}$ B) $\dfrac{40}{3}$ C) $\dfrac{40}{7}$

D) $\dfrac{80}{7}$ E) $\dfrac{80}{3}$

2) If $\angle ABF$ and CBD bisected by $\angle FB$ and $\angle BD$. What is the value of (4m+4n)?

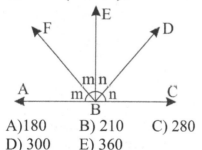

A) 180   B) 210   C) 280
D) 300   E) 360

Use the following figure to answer the questions 3 and question 4.

B=AC, $\angle B = 60^\circ$, $\angle A = 90^\circ$, BE and FC are bisectors.

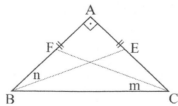

3) What is the value of the (m+n)?

A) 30   B) 36   C) 40
D) 45   E) 60

4) What is the value of the $\angle n - \angle m$?

A) 15   B) 20   C) 25
D) 30   E) 45

5) ABC is the triangle. What is the length of $\overrightarrow{BD}$?

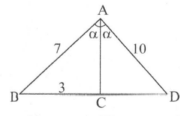

A) $\dfrac{51}{7}$ B) $\dfrac{30}{7}$ C) $\dfrac{7}{30}$

D) $\dfrac{40}{7}$ E) 5

6) The AD is the perpendicular bisector of BC. BD=4 cm, DC=9cm. What is the value of AD?

A) 8
B) 7
C) 6
D) 5
E) 4

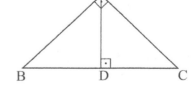

7) $\angle ABD=(3x+10)^o$, $\angle DBC=(2x+15)^o$, what is the value of angle ABD?

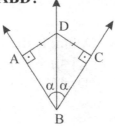

A) 15
B) 14
C) 12
D) 10
E) 5

8) $\angle ABC=134^o$, BD is the bisector. what is the value of $\angle DBC$?

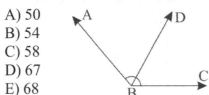

A) 50
B) 54
C) 58
D) 67
E) 68

9) $\overline{AD}$ and $\overline{BE}$ are median. AE and BD are 6, what is the ratio of the line segments of DC and CE?

A) 1

B) 2

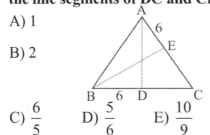

C) $\frac{6}{5}$ D) $\frac{5}{6}$ E) $\frac{10}{9}$

10) $\overline{AD}$ and $\overline{BE}$ are the median. AD=30 and BE=36. What is the ratio of line segments of BK and AK?

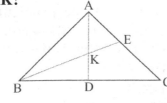

A) $\frac{8}{9}$ B) $\frac{7}{9}$ C) $\frac{8}{7}$

D) $\frac{10}{9}$ E) $\frac{6}{5}$

11) K is the centroid of ABC and KF=7cm. What is the value of KB?

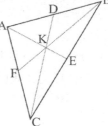

A) 10
B) 12
C) 14
D) 15
E) 16

12) D is the centroid of ABC. AF=12 cm. What is the value of DF?

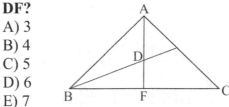

A) 3
B) 4
C) 5
D) 6
E) 7

13) E is the centroid of ABC. $\overline{AD}$ and $\overline{BF}$ are median. DE = 6, what is the value of the AD?

A) 14
B) 18
C) 19
D) 20
E) 21

14) The AD is the bisector of $\triangle ABC$. What is the value of CD?

A) 2   B) 3
C) 4   D) 5.5
E) 6.5

15) The AD is the bisector of $\triangle ABC$. What is the value of BC?

A) 5   B) 6
C) 7   D) 6.6
E) 9

TEST 9
(Polygons)

1) What is the value of ∠C=?

A) 100
B) 110
C) 120
D) 130
E) 140

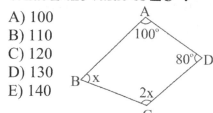

2) What is the value of ∠C-∠D?

A) 39
B) 40
C) 48
D) 51
E) 61

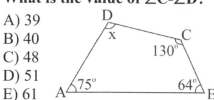

3) What is the value of ∠C - ∠A?

A) 82
B) 73
C) 62
D) 52
E) 42

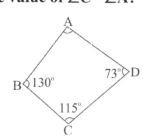

4) What is the value of ∠D+∠B?

A) 120
B) 130
C) 140
D) 145
E) 172

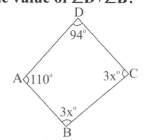

5) ∠A=90°, ∠B=86°, ∠C=2x, ∠D=92°, what is the value of x?

A) 40
B) 42
C) 43
D) 44
E) 46

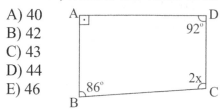

6) What is the value of ∠A+∠C?

A) 180
B) 170
C) 160
D) 150
E) 140

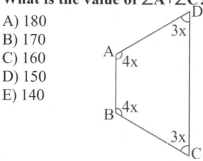

7) ∠D=122°, ∠A=52°, ∠B=66. What is the value of ∠C?

A) 120
B) 122
C) 132
D) 136
E) 140

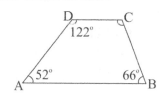

8) What is the value of ∠B-∠C?

A) 40
B) 45
C) 48
D) 55
E) 60

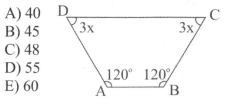

9) ∠A=6x°, ∠B=78°, ∠C=62°, ∠D=8x°, what is the value of ∠D?

A) 90
B) 100.71
C) 110
D) 125.71
E) 145.71

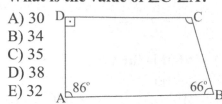

13) ∠D=90°, ∠A=86°, ∠B=66°. What is the value of ∠C-∠A?

A) 30
B) 34
C) 35
D) 38
E) 32

10) AB=BC=DC=ED=EF=FA. What is the value of ∠2A+∠3E?

A) 400
B) 420
C) 480
D) 520
E) 600

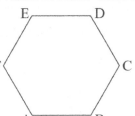

14) What is the value of x?

A) 140
B) 148
C) 150
D) 151
E) 161

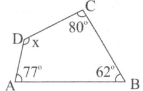

11) ∠A=77°, ∠B=62°, ∠C=80°. What is the value of x?

A) 144
B) 142
C) 141
D) 130
E) 131

15) ∠B=112°, ∠C=122°, ∠D=28°, what is the value of x?

A) 100
B) 98
C) 97
D) 96
E) 95

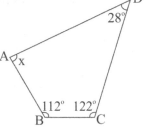

12) ∠A=∠B=76°, ∠C=∠D=4x, what is the value of 4x?

A) 64
B) 78
C) 57
D) 53
E) 104

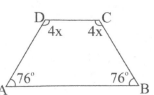

TEST 10

(Midsegment theorem and midpoint formula)

1) **EF∥BC, BC=34cm, what is the value of EF?**

A) 12
B) 13
C) 14
D) 15
E) 17

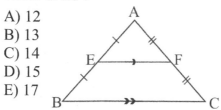

2) **DE∥BC, DE=23cm, what is the value of BC?**

A) 33
B) 34
C) 37
D) 46
E) 44

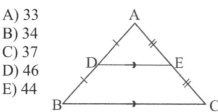

3) **DE∥BC, DE=8x, BC=10x+12, what is the value of BC+DE?**

A) 3
B) 40
C) 43
D) 45
E) 48

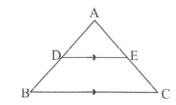

4) **DE∥BC, DE=24, BC=8x+12, what is the value of x?**

A) 8
B) 6
C) 5
D) 4.5
E) 4.3

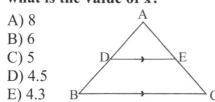

5) **KE=14, KD=12, what is the value of AC+BC?**

A) 50
B) 52
C) 54
D) 58
E) 60

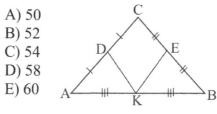

6) **DE=6x+8, what is the value of BC?**

A) 2x+3y
B) 2x+6y
C) 8x+6y
D) 12x+16y
E) 12x+16

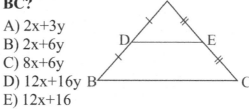

7) **DE=2^9 cm. what is the value of BC?**

A) 2^6
B) 2^8
C) 2^9
D) 2^{10}
E) 2^{13}

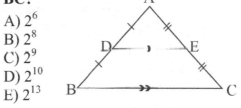

8) **FD=7^x, FE=5^x, what is the value of AC+BA?**

A) $\dfrac{7^x + 9^x}{3}$

B) $\dfrac{7^x + 9^x}{2}$

C) $\dfrac{6^x}{2}$

D) $\dfrac{2^x + 3^x}{4}$ E) $2 \cdot (5^x + 7^x)$

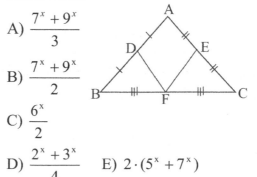

9) Point A is at (–12, –14) and point B is at (–6, 10). What is the midpoint of line segment AB?

A) (–7, –2)
B) (–7, 2)
C) (–9, –2)
D) (–2, 7)
E) (–7, –6)

10) A(–6, 14), B(8, 18). What is the midpoint of a line segment $\overrightarrow{AB}$?

A) (1, 16)
B) (–2, 8)
C) (7, –1)
D) (–1, 8)
E) (–2, 8)

11) K is the midpoint of AB. The coordinated K(–5, 5) and A(7, 3) are given. What are the coordinates of point B?

A) (–17,7)
B) (-16, –9)
C) (10, 4)
D) (–8, 4)
E) (–7, –6)

12) What is the midpoint of the straight line segment joining the points (–5, 9) and (–7, 11)?

A) (–5, –8)
B) (–5, 10)
C) (10, –5)
D) (5, 10)
E) (–6, 10)

13) A (–2, 4), B(9, 6), C(6, –5). What is the midpoint of AB?

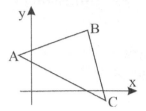

A) (1, 3)   B) $\left(\dfrac{7}{2}, 5\right)$

C) $\left(2, 6\dfrac{1}{2}\right)$ D) $\left(3, 6\dfrac{1}{2}\right)$

E) $\left(6\dfrac{1}{2}, 2\right)$

14) A(–9, 7), B(–2, –6) and C(6, –2). What is the midpoint of BC?

A) (–1, –6)
B) (–1, –7)
C) (1, –6)
D) (–6, 1)
E) (2, –4)

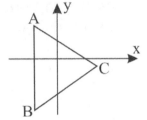

15) A(–4, 6), B(–2, 0), AC=CD=DE=EB, What are the coordinates of E?

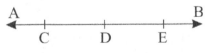

A) (12, -2)   B) (12, 2)
C) (-2, 12)   D) (6, 12)
E) $\left(\dfrac{-5}{2}, \dfrac{3}{2}\right)$

TEST 11

(Parallelograms)

1) ∠A=54°, what is the value of ∠B−∠C?

   A) 72
   B) 73
   C) 74
   D) 75
   E) 76

   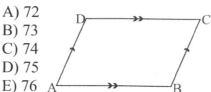

2) ∠B=135° and ∠A=3x, what is the value of 2x?

   A) 40
   B) 30
   C) 28
   D) 14
   E) 13

   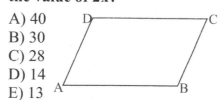

3) How many parallelograms in the figure?

   A) 6
   B) 7
   C) 8
   D) 9
   E) 10

   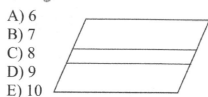

4) ABCD is a parallelogram. ∠B=108° and ∠C=3x, what is the value of 2x?

   A) 24
   B) 30
   C) 44
   D) 48
   E) 52

   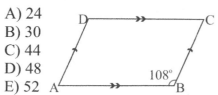

5) ∠C=48°, ∠A=4m, ∠B=3n, what is the value of m+n?

   A) 32
   B) 42
   C) 54
   D) 56
   E) 68

   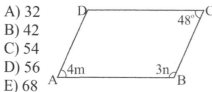

6) ABCD is parallelogram. ∠CBE=66°, what is the value of ∠2D−∠A?

   A) 132
   B) 142
   C) 152
   D) 162
   E) 173

   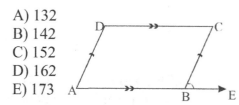

7) ABCD is parallelogram. AB=27, BC=$\sqrt{28}$, what is the value of x+y?

   A) $6+\sqrt{6}$
   B) $8+\sqrt{6}$
   C) $4+\sqrt{3}$
   D) $3+\sqrt{5}$
   E) $9+\sqrt{7}$

   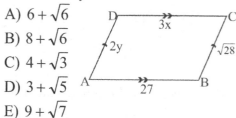

8) ABCD is parallelogram. AB=8x, BC=4y, what is the value of 4m+3n?

   A) 30
   B) 44
   C) 33
   D) 34
   E) 36

   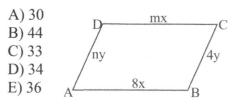

9) If $\angle A = 123°$, what is the value of 3x?

A) 165
B) 166
C) 171
D) 182
E) 183

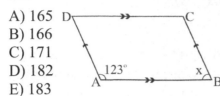

10) ABCD is the parallelogram. $\angle A = 10n$, $\angle B = 6m$, what is the value of 5n+3m?

A) 90
B) 60
C) 55
D) 45
E) 30

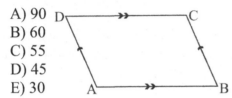

11) Find the perimeter ABCD. AB=x+6, what is the value of BC=2+x?

A) 28+6x
B) 4x+16
C) 30+6x
D) 4x+18
E) 16

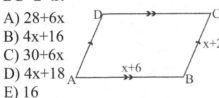

12) ABCD is the parallelogram. AB=2^9cm, BC=2^6cm. The perimeter of a parallelogram ABCD is $2^A \cdot B$, what is the value of A+B?

A) 10
B) 11
C) 12
D) 13
E) 16

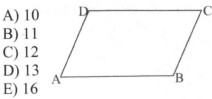

13) AB=6, BF=FC=4, what is the sum all perimeter of parallelograms?

A) 52
B) 74
C) 84
D) 90
E) 68

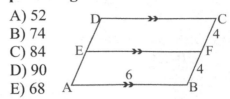

14) ABCD is the parallelogram. $DE = \sqrt{14}$, $EC = \sqrt{26}$, what is the value of AC+BD?

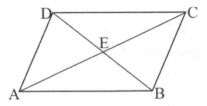

A) $3\sqrt{14} + 3\sqrt{26}$
B) $4\sqrt{14} + 4\sqrt{26}$
C) $4\sqrt{3} + 4\sqrt{6}$
D) $2\sqrt{14} + 2\sqrt{26}$
E) $4\sqrt{6} + 3\sqrt{5}$

15) AE=3^x, BE=2^x, (AC)·(BD)=$m \cdot 6^{nx}$, what is the value of m+n?

A) 2
B) 3
C) 4
D) 5
E) 6

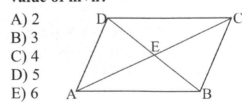

TEST 12
(Rhombuses, Rectangles, and Squares)

1) ABCD is the rhombuses. AB=6y, BC=48, what is the value of y?

A) 8
B) 9
C) 10
D) 12
E) 14

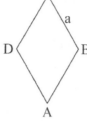

2) ABCD is the square. AL=LB=BE=EC. How many squares in the figure?

A) 5
B) 6
C) 7
D) 8
E) 10

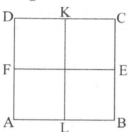

3) ABCD is the square. ∠BAC=2x, ∠ABC=3y, what is the value of y–x?

A) 7.20
B) 7.5
C) 8
D) 8.5
E) 9

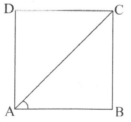

4) ABCD is the rhombus. ∠A=68°, ∠C=2x, what is the value of x?

A) 23
B) 24
C) 30
D) 34
E) 32

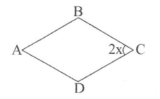

5) ABCD is the parallelogram. AC=14, BD=12, what is the value of 2AE–BE=?

A) 4
B) 5
C) 6
D) 7
E) 8

6) ABCD is the rectangle. B=6x+6, DC=42, AD=30, BC=5y+5, what is the value of 2x+3y?

A) 30
B) 28
C) 26
D) 25
E) 27

7) ABCD is the rectangle. KLMN is the square. AB=10, BC=8, KL=9, what is the ratio of the perimeter of square KLMN and the perimeter of rectangle ABCD?

A) 9/7   B) $\dfrac{3\sqrt{7}}{2}$ C) $\dfrac{1}{\sqrt{7}}$

D) 9/5   E) 1

8) ABCD is the rhombus. KLMN is the square. BC=7^{x}cm, KL=14^x, what is the ratio of the perimeter of square KLMN and the perimeter of rhombus ABCD?

A) 1
B) 2
C) $\dfrac{1}{3^x}$
D) 3^x
E) 2^x

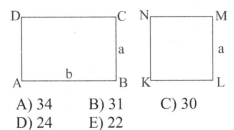

9) ABCD is a rectangle. KLMN is square. If the sum of the perimeter of rectangle ABCD and square KLMN is 68cm. What is the value of 3a+b?

A) 34   B) 31   C) 30
D) 24   E) 22

10) ABCD is the square. AB=7^x, KLMN is the rhombus. KL=7. What is the ratio of the perimeter of square ABCD and the perimeter of rhombus KLMN?

A) 7^x
B) 7^{x+1}
C) 7^{x-1}
D) 7^{2x}
E) 7

11) ABCD is the square. AE=12cm, what is the value of BD?

A) 12
B) 16
C) 18
D) 24
E) 30

12) ABCD is the rhombus AC=24cm, BD=10cm, what is the value of AB?

A) 15   B) 14
C) 13   D) 12
E) 16

13) ABCD is the square. EC=9$\sqrt{2}$ cm, What is the perimeter of the square ABCD?

A) 18
B) 24
C) 36
D) 45
E) 72

14) ABCD is the rectangle. AB=4, BC=2, what is the ratio of the perimeter of rectangle ABCD and the sum of the diagonals AC and BD?

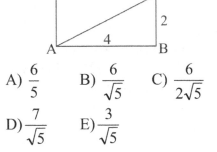

A) $\dfrac{6}{5}$ B) $\dfrac{6}{\sqrt{5}}$ C) $\dfrac{6}{2\sqrt{5}}$

D) $\dfrac{7}{\sqrt{5}}$ E) $\dfrac{3}{\sqrt{5}}$

15) ABCD is the rectangle. AB=20, BC=15, what is the ratio of the length AC and BC?

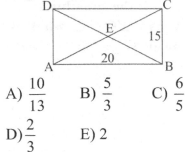

A) $\dfrac{10}{13}$ B) $\dfrac{5}{3}$ C) $\dfrac{6}{5}$

D) $\dfrac{2}{3}$ E) 2

TEST 13

(Trapezoid)

1) ABCD is an isosceles trapezoid. ∠A=46°. What is the value of ∠B?

A) 123
B) 128
C) 134
D) 132
E) 46

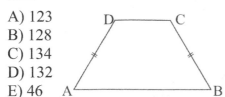

2) EF is the mid-segment. DC=11 cm, AB=17cm, what is the value of EF?

A) 10
B) 11
C) 12
D) 13
E) 14

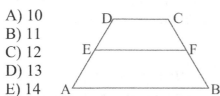

3) ∠D=48°. What is the value of ∠B?

A) 114
B) 124
C) 132
D) 144
E) 148

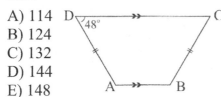

4) EF is the mid-segment. DC=4x+6, AB=6x+8, what is the value of EF?

A) 4x+7
B) 7x+4
C) 6x+6
D) 5x+5
E) 5x+7

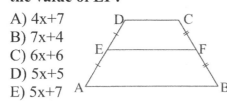

5) EF is the mid-segment. BC=12, EF=18, what is the value of AD?

A) 18
B) 19
C) 20
D) 24
E) 26

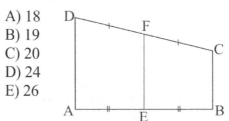

6) AB=6x+6, DC=2x+2, EF=16, what is the value of x?

A) 2
B) 3
C) 4
D) 5
E) 6

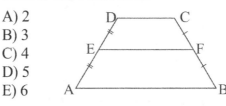

7) ∠B=132°, ∠D=42°, what is the value of ∠A?

A) 65
B) 103
C) 105
D) 106
E) 93

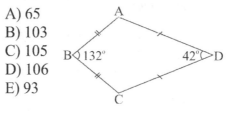

8) ∠A=82°, ∠B=110°, what is the value of ∠C?

A) 50
B) 52
C) 56
D) 58
E) 60

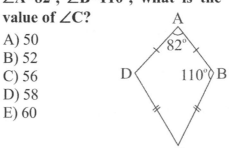

9) $\angle D=48°$. What is the value of $\angle C$?

A) 158
B) 142
C) 132
D) 48
E) 40

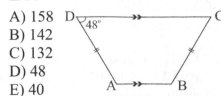

12) ABCD is the trapezoid. AD=BC, what is the value of $\angle D-\angle A$?

A) 36
B) 37
C) 38
D) 39
E) 40

10) ABCD is the trapezoid. DC∥AB, DE∥BC, what is the value of n?

A) 81
B) 84
C) 71
D) 61
E) 58

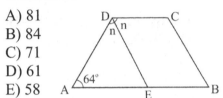

13) ABCD is the trapezoid. EF is the mid-segment. AB=8m, DC=6n, what is the value of EF?

A) 6m+8n
B) 3m+4n
C) 8m+6n
D) 7mn
E) 4m+3n

11) ABCD is the trapezoid. EF is the mid-segment.

If $\dfrac{DC}{AB}=\dfrac{3}{7}$ what is the value of

$$\dfrac{EF}{AB+DC}=?$$

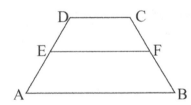

A) $\dfrac{5}{11}$ B) $\dfrac{4}{11}$ C) $\dfrac{1}{2}$

D) $\dfrac{11}{7}$ E) $\dfrac{13}{6}$

14) ABCD is the trapezoid. EF is the mid-segment, AB=5^{2x+2}, DC=5^{x+1}, what is the value of EF?

A) $2^{2x+1}+2^x$
B) 2^{2x+1}
C) $(5^{2x+2}+5^{x+1})/2$
D) $(2^{2x}+2^{3x}$
E) $2^{3x}+2^1$

15) ABCD is the trapezoid. AD=12cm, BC=8cm, EF=16 cm, what is the perimeter ABCD?

A) 52
B) 60
C) 64
D) 68
E) 70

TEST 14

(Areas of triangles and Quadrilaterals)

1) ABC is the triangle. AB=14, DC=6, what is the area of triangle ABC?

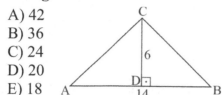

A) 42
B) 36
C) 24
D) 20
E) 18

2) ABC is the triangle. AB=18, BC=8, what is the area of triangle ABC?

A) 60
B) 72
C) 46
D) 48
E) 50

3) AB=x+6, BC=6. The area of the triangle ABC is 48 cm². What is the value of x=?

A) 2
B) 3
C) 4
D) 5
E) 10

4) The area of the triangle ABC is 48 cm². AD=16, what is the value of BC?

A) 3
B) 4
C) 5
D) 6
E) 7

5) The area of the triangle ABC is 24 cm². What is the value of x?

A) 2
B) 3
C) 4
D) 5
E) 6

6) AB=AC=BC=12 cm, what is the area of triangle ABC?

A) 144
B) $25\sqrt{3}$
C) $25\sqrt{3}$
D) $36\sqrt{3}$
E) 30

7) ABC is the triangle. ∠A=∠C=45°. The area of the triangle ABC is 16 cm². What is the value of BC?

A) $4\sqrt{2}$
B) $2\sqrt{3}$
C) $2\sqrt{5}$
D) $2\sqrt{6}$
E) $3\sqrt{6}$

8) ∠B=α=30°, AB=8, BC=10, what is the area of triangle ABC?

A) 12
B) 16
C) 20
D) 28
E) 48

9) ABC is the triangle.
BD=DE=EC. The area of the
triangle ABD is 7cm^2, what is
the area of triangle ABC?

A) 12
B) 16
C) 21
D) 24
E) 36

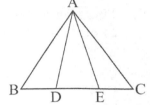

10) $\dfrac{BD}{DC} = \dfrac{4}{7}$, The area of the

triangle ABD is 16cm^2, what is
the area of triangle ABC?

A) 44cm^2
B) 38cm^2
C) 55cm^2
D) 65cm^2
E) 66cm^2

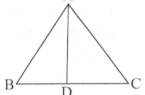

11) ABC is the triangle. AB=16.
The area of the triangle ABD is
48. What is the value of DC?

A) 10
B) 9
C) 8
D) 7
E) 6

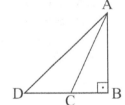

12) ABC is the triangle. AC=20 ,
BD=8 , BC=10, AE=?

A) 6,6
B) 8,8
C) 11
D) 12
E) 16

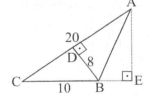

13) The area of the triangle ADE is
8cm^2, what is the area of
triangle ABC?

A) 16
B) 32
C) 24
D) 28
E) 36

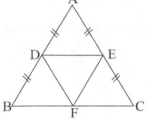

14) ABC is the triangle. The area of
the triangle ABC is 70 cm^2,

$\dfrac{CD}{DB} = \dfrac{2}{5}$, what is the area of

triangle ACD?

A) 20
B) 35
C) 40
D) 45
E) 48

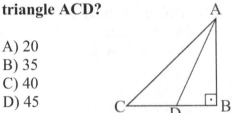

15) BD$= \sqrt{6}$, DC$= \sqrt{12}$, what is the
ratio of the area of triangle
ABD and the area of triangle
ADC?

A) 1
B) 2
C) $\sqrt{2}$
D) $\dfrac{1}{\sqrt{2}}$
E) $\dfrac{1}{3}$

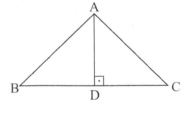

TEST 15
(Area of the Square)

1) ABCD is the square. AC=16cm. What is the area of the square ABCD?

A) 50
B) 80
C) 100
D) 150
E) 128

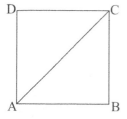

5) ABCD is the square. AB=5. What is the area of the square ABCD?

A) 5   B) 20
C) 25   D) 55
E) 65

2) ABCD is the square. The perimeter of square ABCD is 60cm. What is the area of the square ABCD?

A) 121
B) 144
C) 134
D) 440
E) 225

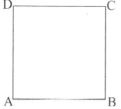

6) ABCD is the square. AE=5cm. What is the area of the square ABCD?

A) 30
B) 32
C) 36
D) 50
E) 64

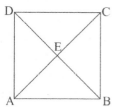

3) ABCD is the square. The perimeter ABCD is 12. What is the area of the square ABCD?

A) 2
B) 4
C) 6
D) 9
E) 12

7) ABCD is the square. The area of the triangle BEC is 18cm^2. What is the area of triangle DAB?

A) 36
B) 56
C) 66
D) 72
E) 77

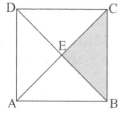

4) ABCD is the square. AB=11^{x}cm. What is the area of the square ABCD?

A) 11^{3x}
B) 11^{2x}
C) 4·11^x
D) 8·11^x
E) 121^{2x}

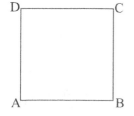

8) ABCD is the square. AB=7^{a}cm. What is the perimeter of square ABCD?

A) 4·7^a B) 7^{-a}
C) 4·2^a D) 7a
E) 4a

9) ABCD is the square. Δ(ABE)=72cm². What is the perimeter of square ABCD?

A) 20 cm²
B) 48 cm²
C) 42 cm²
D) 44 cm²
E) 56 cm²

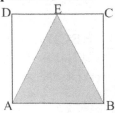

10) ABCD is the square. The area of the triangle BEC is 25 cm². What is the perimeter of the square ABCD?

A) 40
B) 50
C) 52
D) 54
E) 60

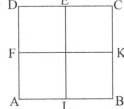

11) ABCD is the square. AL=LB=BK=KC. AD=10 cm. What is the sum of the all area of the squares?

A) 100
B) 120
C) 140
D) 160
E) 180

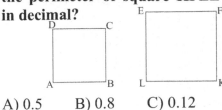

12) ABCD and KFEL are the squares. The area of the square ABCD is 144cm²and the area of the square KFEL is 225cm². What is the ratio of the perimeter of square ABCD and the perimeter of square KFEL in decimal?

A) 0.5   B) 0.8   C) 0.12
D) 0.18   E) 0.15

13) ABCD and EFKL are the squares. AB=14cm. EF=8cm. What is the shaded area?

A) 96
B) 120
C) 132
D) 112
E) 128

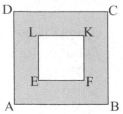

14) ABCD and EFKL are the squares. Perimeter ABCD is 44, and perimeter EFKL is the 12cm. What is the ratio of the area of square ABCD and the area of square EFKL?

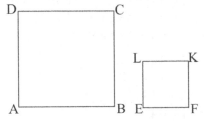

A) 8   B) 6   C) $\frac{9}{121}$

D) $\frac{121}{9}$ E) $\frac{9}{144}$

15) ABCD and LKFE are squares. DB=6 cm, FL=4 cm. What is the ratio of the area of square ABCD and the area of square LKFE?

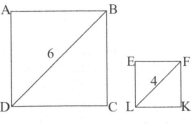

A) $\frac{48}{17}$ B) $\frac{9}{4}$ C) $\frac{9}{7}$

D) $\frac{16}{65}$ E) $\frac{7}{2}$

TEST 16

(Area and Perimeter of the Rectangle)

1) ABCD is the rectangle. B=x+6, BC=x+2, what is the perimeter of rectangle ABCD?

A) 4x+8
B) 4x+16
C) 4x+12
D) 4x+4
E) 12x+4

2) ABCD is the rectangle. AB=4x, BC=3x, perimeter ABCD is 70 cm. What is the area of rectangle ABCD?

A) 300
B) 280
C) 260
D) 240
E) 230

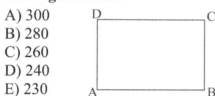

3) ABCD is the rectangle. AB=3x, BC=12. What is the area of rectangle ABCD?

A) 18x
B) 36x
C) 12x
D) 18
E) 36

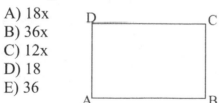

4) ABCD is the rectangle. Area of ABCD is the 72 cm². What is the perimeter of rectangle ABCD?

A) 30
B) 32
C) 36
D) 40
E) 45

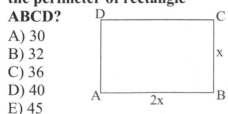

5) ABCD is the rectangle. BC=5, AC=13. What is the area of rectangle ABCD?

A) 32
B) 44
C) 54
D) 60
E) 68

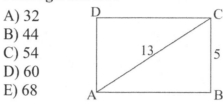

6) ABCD is the rectangle. BC=12, AB=16. What is the perimeter of triangle BAC?

A) 40
B) 42
C) 45
D) 46
E) 48

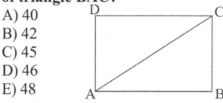

7) AB=12, BC=10. What is the ratio of the area of the rectangle ABCD and the area of the triangle ABC?

A) 1
B) 2
C) 3
D) 4
E) $\frac{2}{3}$

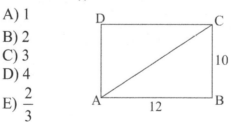

8) A rectangle has edges with lengths of 2 cm and 4 cm. What is the length of a diagonal of the rectangle?

A) 34   B) 17   C) $\sqrt{34}$
D) $\sqrt{32}$ E) $\sqrt{20}$

9) The lengths of two sides of a rectangle are in the ratio 1:4. What is the area of the rectangle if its perimeter is 20 cm?

A) 16   B) 18   C) 20

D) 22   E) 24

10) AE=5, EC=12, ∠DEC=90°. What is the value of DE?

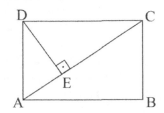

A) $\sqrt{6}$ B) $2\sqrt{6}$ C) $2\sqrt{15}$

D) $2\sqrt{5}$ E) 4

11) AB=6, BC=5, DC=7. What is the ratio of the area of the triangle ABD and the area of the triangle BCD?

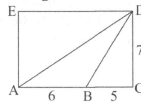

A) $\dfrac{5}{7}$ B) $\dfrac{6}{5}$ C) $\dfrac{5}{3}$

D) $\dfrac{3}{5}$ E) $\dfrac{4}{5}$

12) ABCD is the rectangle. AB=6, BC=4cm. The area of triangle ABD is 30cm². What is the area of triangle ADE?

A) 20 cm²
B) 32 cm²
C) 45 cm²
D) 36 cm²
E) 52 cm²

13) ABCD and LEFK are rectangles. AB=8, BC=4n, LE=3x, EF=2y. What is the area of the shaded region?

A) 32n-xy
B) 6xy-32n
C) 12n-8xy
D) 16n-6xy
E) 32n-6xy

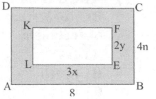

14) ABCD and EFKL are rectangles. AB=4m, BC=3n, EF=m, KF=n. What are the ratio of the perimeter rectangle ABCD and the perimeter of rectangle LEFK?

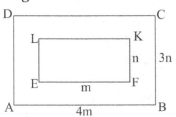

A) $\dfrac{4m+3n}{m+n}$ B) 4m+3n

C) 2m+2n   D) $\dfrac{8m+3n}{2m+n}$

E) 2m+3n

15) ABCD is the rectangle. AE=EC. What is the value of ∠ECB?

A) 23
B) 44
C) 46
D) 50
E) 54

TEST 17

(Area and Perimeter of the Parallelogram)

1) ABCD is the parallelogram. $\angle BDC=32^0$, $\angle ADB=72^0$. What is the value of $\angle ABC$?

A) 104
B) 106
C) 108
D) 110
E) 112

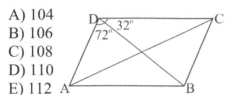

2) ABCD is the parallelogram. AB=2x, DC=18, BC=2m, AD=14, AE=8. What is the value of (x+m+a)?

A) 24
B) 29
C) 28
D) 27
E) 25

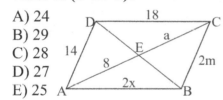

3) ABCD is the parallelogram. AB=6y, DC=24cm, AD=16cm, BC=4x–4. What is the value of x+y?

A) 9
B) 10
C) 11
D) 12
E) 13

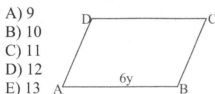

4) ABCD is the parallelogram. $\angle A=4x^0$, $\angle D=8x^0$. What is the value of x?

A) 40
B) 36
C) 30
D) 25
E) 15

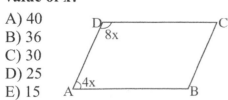

5) ABCD is the parallelogram. AB=6x–6, DC=30. What is the value of (x^2+4)?

A) 34
B) 38
C) 40
D) 44
E) 48

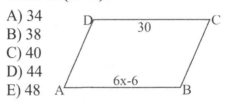

6) What is the area of the parallelogram with base 14 cm and height 8 cm?

A) 112
B) 124
C) 134
D) 155
E) 166

7) ABCD is the parallelogram. AB=12, ED=6. What is the area of parallelogram ABCD?

A) 20
B) 72
C) 36
D) 40
E) 80

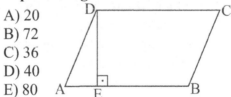

8) ABCD is the parallelogram. BC=10cm, DE=13 cm, AB=12cm. What is the area of parallelogram ABCD?

A) 44
B) 88
C) 96
D) 98
E) 130

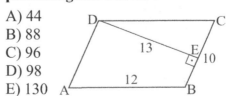

9) ABCD is the parallelogram. AB=18cm, DE=12cm, DF=16cm. What is the value of AD?

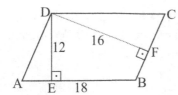

A) $\dfrac{27}{7}$ B) $\dfrac{27}{2}$ C) $\dfrac{80}{14}$

D) $\dfrac{80}{7}$ E) $\dfrac{80}{17}$

10) ABCD is the parallelogram. ∠A=72°. What is the value of (x–y)?

A) 50
B) 48
C) 36
D) 44
E) 42

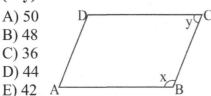

11) The ratio of the side of a parallelogram is 13:17. What is the least possible integer value of its perimeter?

A) 48   B) 50   C) 56
D) 60   E) 66

12) ABCD is the parallelogram. The area of triangle ADE is 13cm². What is the area of triangle ABC?

A) 36
B) 26
C) 18
D) 16
E) 9

13) What is the area of the parallelogram with base 16 cm and height 4cm?

A) 64   B) 54   C) 44
D) 42   E) 36

14) ABCD is the parallelogram. AK=14, BK=8. What is the ratio of AC and BD?

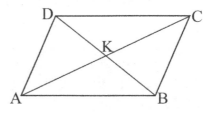

A) $\dfrac{12}{5}$ B) $\dfrac{13}{6}$ C) $\dfrac{9}{8}$

D) $\dfrac{7}{9}$ E) $\dfrac{7}{4}$

15) ABCD is the parallelogram. The ratio of AB and BC is 7 to 3. The perimeter of parallelogram ABCD is 80 cm. What is the value of BC?

A) 11
B) 12
C) 13
D) 14
E) 15

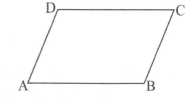

TEST 18

(Area and Perimeter of the Rhombus)

1) What is the perimeter of a rhombus with an edge length of 12 cm?

   A) 26   B) 39   C) 48
   D) 52   E) 62

2) The perimeter of a rhombus is 44 cm. What is the side of the rhombus?

   A) 11   B) 13   C) 14
   D) 15   E) 20

3) The perimeter of a rhombus is 12x, what is each side of the rhombus?

   A) 3x   B) 3   C) 24x
   D) 24   E) 12x

4) What is the area of a rhombus with diagonal lengths 8 cm and 6 cm?

   A) 14   B) 18   C) 20
   D) 24   E) 30

5) The perimeter of a rhombus is 4a cm. What is each side of the rhombus?

   A) 4a   B) 4^a C) a
   D) 2^a E) 2a

6) The diagonals of a rhombus are 12 cm and 16 cm, what is the length of its one side?

   A) 8   B) 9   C) 10
   D) 12   E) 13

7) The side length of a rhombus is 10cm. What is the area of the rhombus if its smaller angle is 45°?

   A) $50\sqrt{2}$ B) $60\sqrt{2}$ C) $70\sqrt{2}$
   D) $80\sqrt{2}$ E) $25\sqrt{2}$

8) The diagonal length of a rhombus is 6 cm and 8 cm. What is the side of the rhombus?

   A) 13   B) 12   C) $\frac{13}{2}$
   D) 6   E) 5

9) What is the perimeter of a rhombus with diagonal lengths 12 cm and 16 cm?

   A) 30   B) 40   C) 50
   D) 60   E) 65

10) ABCD is the rhombus. AC=10, BD=8. What is the value of BC?

   A) $5\sqrt{3}$ B) $3\sqrt{5}$
   C) $4\sqrt{3}$ D) $\sqrt{41}$
   E) 5

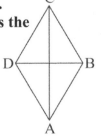

11) ABCD is the rhombus. BC=12cm, EF=8cm, ∠DFE=90°. What is the area of rhombus ABCD?

A) 63
B) 72
C) 70
D) 64
E) 96

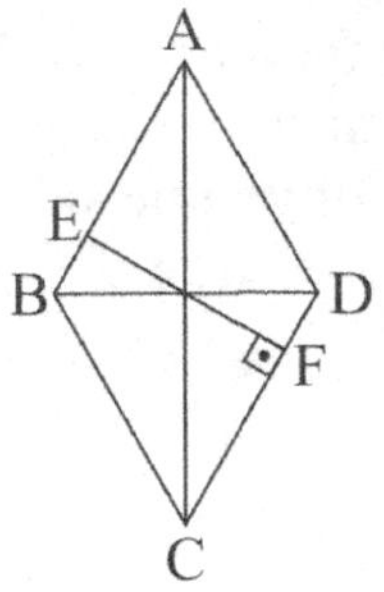

12) What is the perimeter of a rhombus with side lengths 16?

A) 78　　B) 70　　C) 64
D) 32　　E) 30

13) What is the area of a rhombus with side lengths 8 and altitude 4 cm?

A) $10\sqrt{2}$　B) $20\sqrt{2}$　C) 32
D) 20　　E) 24

14) What is the side of a rhombus with diagonal lengths 12cm and 8cm?

A) $3\sqrt{3}$　B) $4\sqrt{3}$　C) $6\sqrt{3}$
D) $8\sqrt{13}$　E) $2\sqrt{13}$

15) The rhombus area is 48. The side is 6 cm. What is the altitude of the rhombus?

A) 8　　B) 9　　C) 10
D) 12　　E) $4\sqrt{5}$

TEST 19

(Rigid motion in a Plane and Reflections)

Use the following figure for questions 1-2.

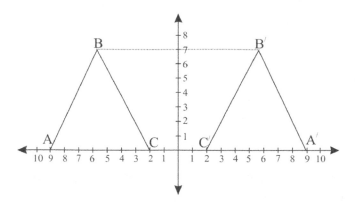

1) What is the coordinate A′=?

   A) (9, 7)   B) (8, 7)
   C) (7, 10)   D) (11, 4)
   E) (9, 8)

2) What is the coordinate B′=?

   A) (6, 6)   B) (5.5, 7) C) (7, 6)
   D) (7, 8)   E) (7, 4)

Use the following figure for questions 3-4.

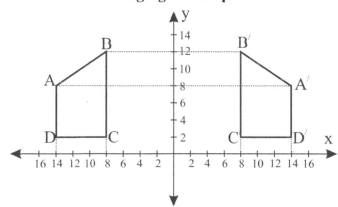

3) If the trapezoid ABCD reflected over y-axis, what is the coordinates A′?

   A) (14, 12)   B) (12, 14)
   C) (14, 8)   D) (10, 8)
   E) (9, 8)

4) If the trapezoid ABCD reflected over y-axis, what is the coordinates B′?

   A) (8, 2)   B) (8, 4)
   C) (8, 12)   D) (12, 8)
   E) (12, 4)

5) If K(6, 10) is reflected in the line y=6, then K/=?

A) (4, 2)   B) (4, 6)
C) (4, 8)   D) (4, 0)
E) (6, 2)

6) If N(14, –6) is reflected in the line x=8, then N/=?

A) (0, 4)   B) (2, –6)
C) (4, 0)   D) (–4, 0)
E) (6, –2)

7) If A(8, 6) is reflected in the line x=3, then A/=?

A) (3, 3)   B) (3, –3)
C) (–3, 3)   D) (–2, 6)
E) (6, 4)

Use the following figure for questions 8-9.

Given that the diagram shows a reflection in a line

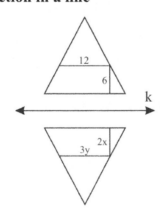

8) What is the value of y?

A) 1   B) 2   C) 4
D) 5   E) 6

9) What is the value of (x+y)?

A) 10   B) 9   C) 8
D) 7   E) 6

Use the following figure for questions 10-11.

Given that the diagram shows a reflection in a line:

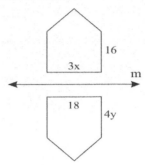

10) What is the value of x?

A) 10   B) 9   C) 8
D) 7   E) 6

11) What is the value of 2(x+y)?

A) 20   B) 19   C) 18
D) 17   E) 16

12) What is the coordinates of A(10, 6) reflected in the line y=4?

A) (8, 4) B) (2, -6) C) (10, 2)
D) (0, 8) E) (0, 4)

13) What is the coordinates of M(–6, 12) reflected in the y-axis? M/=?

A) (-6, -12)   B) (–4, 10)
C) (10, 4)   D) (–10, 4)
E) (4, 8)

14) What is the coordinates of M(–4, 8) reflected in the x-axis. M′=?

A) (3, 3) B) (3, 4) C) (7, 4)
D) (3, 7) E) (8, 4)

15) Find the coordinates of N(5, 4) reflected B(0, 0). N/=?

A) (–3, –4)   B) (–3, 4)
C) (–4, 3)   D) (–5, –4)
E) (–3, 6)

TEST 20

(Translation and Vectors)

Use the coordinate notation to describe the translation.

1) **Eight units to the right and four units down. (x, y) →?**
   A) (x+8, y–4)   B) (x+7, y–3)
   C) (x+3, y–7)   D) (x+3, y+7)
   E) (x–3, y+4)

2) **Seven units up and 13 units to the right. (x, y) →?**
   A) (x+12, y+6)   B) (x+7, y–13)
   C) (x+6, y+12)   D) (x+13, y+7)
   E) (x+12, y+4)

3) **12 units down and eight units to the left. (x, y) →?**
   A) (x+10, y+7)   B) (x–10, y–10)
   C) (x–8, y–12)   D) (x+6, y+6)
   E) (x–10, y–10)

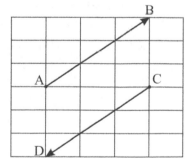

Name the vector and write its component form.

4) A) $\overrightarrow{AB}$; (4, 2)   B) $\overrightarrow{AB}$; (3, 3)
   C) $\overrightarrow{AB}$; (2, 4)   D) $\overrightarrow{AB}$; (3, –3)
   E) $\overrightarrow{AB}$; (–2, –2)

5) A) $\overrightarrow{CD}$; (–3, –3) B) $\overrightarrow{CD}$; (3, 3)
   C) $\overrightarrow{CD}$; (4, 3)   D) $\overrightarrow{CD}$; (–3, 3)
   E) $\overrightarrow{CD}$; (2, –3)

6) **Five units to the left six units up. (x, y) →?**
   A) (x+12, y+6)   B) (x+7, y–13)
   C) (x+6, y+12)   D) (x-5, y+6)
   E) (x+12, y+4)

7) **Consider the translation that defined by the coordinate notation (x, y)→(x+6; y–4). What is the image of (5, 9)?**
   A) (8, 4)   B) (8, 0)
   C) (8, 3)   D) (8, 2)
   E) (11, 5)

8) **(x, y) → (x+9; y+5). What is the image of (5, 6)?**
   A) (14, 11)   B) (10, 6)
   C) (7, 10)   D) (8, 5)
   E) (8, 6)

9) **(x, y) → (x+6; y+8). The point (8, 7) will be?**
   A) (10, 4)   B) (10, 2)
   C) (12, 10)   D) (10, 9)
   E) (14, 15)

10) Use the translation
(x, y) → (x-5, y+5). What is the image of A(10, 10)?
A) (9, 8) B) (5, 15)
C) (5, 10) D) (6, 18)
E) (18, 10)

11) The vector A(-5, -3) is translated six units right and 11 units down. What are the coordinates of the endpoint?
A) (1, -14) B) (1, 8)
C) (2, 12) D) (3, 10)
E) (6, 8)

12) Describe the translation of eight units to the left and 10 unit up using a vector.
A) (-6, -8) B) (-6, 8)
C) (-8, 10) D) (-6, 7)
E) (-8, -6)

13) Describe in words the distance and direction of the translation represented by the vector <6, -14>.
A) 6 units down and 14 units up
B) 6 units right and 14 units down
C) 14 units left and 6 units down
D) 6 units left and 14 units down
E) 14 units up and 6 units down

14) Use the translation
(x, y) → (x+6, y-4). What is the image of A(12; 14)?
A) (9, 8) B) (12, 10)
C) (10, 8) D) (6, 18)
E) (18, 10)

15) Use the translation (x, y) → (x-6, y+2).   A(13; -6)→?
A) (-12, 10) B) (-12, 4)
C) (7, 2) D) (7, -4)
E) (-2, 7)

TEST 21
(Similar Triangles)

1) △ABC~△DEC, DE=8 cm, AB=32, AC=48. What is the value of DC?

A) 6.6
B) 7.5
C) 8.6
D) 9.5
E) 9.6

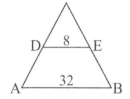

2) The triangles shown are similar. What is the value of x?

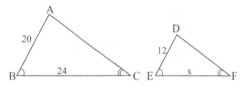

A) 16.4   B) 15.4   C) 14.4
D) 13.3   E) 12.4

3) AB∥DC and ∠A=44°, ∠CED=32°, What is the value of ∠C?

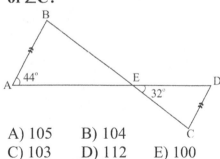

A) 105   B) 104
C) 103   D) 112   E) 100

4) DE∥BC and AD=8, DB=11, EC=x+3. What is the value of x?

A) 11
B) 10
C) 9
D) 8
E) 7

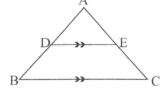

5) AD=6, BD=8, AE=10. What is the value of EC?

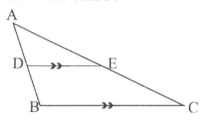

A) $\frac{192}{13}$ B) $\frac{191}{12}$ C) $\frac{189}{13}$

D) $\frac{188}{15}$ E) $\frac{40}{3}$

6) AD=10, DB=4, AE=8. What is the value of EC?

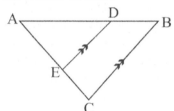

A) $\frac{57}{3}$ B) $\frac{57}{4}$ C) $\frac{56}{3}$

D) $\frac{16}{5}$ E) 7.2

7) DE∥BC and AD=9, DB=13.5, AE=10. What is the value of EC?

A) 15
B) 12
C) 9
D) 8
E) 5

8) What is the value of x?

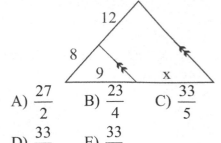

A) $\dfrac{27}{2}$ B) $\dfrac{23}{4}$ C) $\dfrac{33}{5}$

D) $\dfrac{33}{2}$ E) $\dfrac{33}{4}$

9) DE∥BC and AE=10, AC=15, AD=9. What is the value of AB?

A) 10
B) 12
C) 12.5
D) 13.5
E) 15

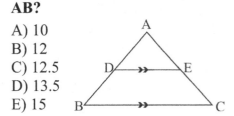

10) Triangle ABC and triangle DEF are similar. BC=5cm and EF=12cm. The area of the triangle ABC is 15cm². What is the area of triangle DEF?

A) 9
B) 15
C) 20
D) 25
E) 36

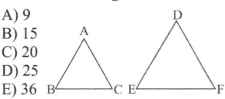

11) What is the value of x?

A) $\dfrac{9}{2}$

B) $\dfrac{9}{4}$

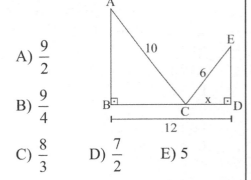

C) $\dfrac{8}{3}$ D) $\dfrac{7}{2}$ E) 5

12) AD=14, DC=18, BC=20. What is the value of DE?

A) 3
B) 4.75
C) 5
D) 4.5
E) 8.75

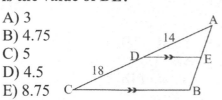

13) DE∥BC, DE is the mid-segment. The area of the triangle ADE is 9cm². What is the area of the triangle ABC?

A) 18
B) 24
C) 30
D) 36
E) 42

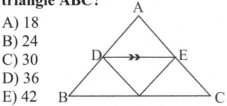

14) DE and FE are the midpoint segments. DE=8cm, FE=6cm. What is the value of AB+BC?

A) 20
B) 18
C) 17
D) 16
E) 28

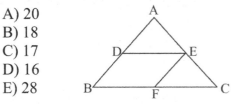

15) AE=6, EC=18. What is the relationship between x and y?

A) x=y
B) x=2y
C) x=3y
D) y=4x
E) y=3x

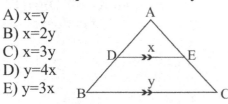

TEST 22

(The Pythagorean Theorem)

1) What is the value of the length of a hypotenuse?

A) $\sqrt{43}$
B) $\sqrt{55}$
C) $\sqrt{65}$
D) $\sqrt{66}$
E) $\sqrt{72}$

2) $\angle A=90^{\circ}$, AB=12, AC=5. What is the value of x?

A) 2.33
B) 2.66
C) 3.33
D) 4.33
E) 5.33

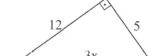

3) $\angle B=90^{\circ}$, AB=$\frac{1}{7}$, BC=$\frac{3}{7}$. What is the value of AC?

A) $\frac{\sqrt{10}}{4}$
B) $\frac{\sqrt{10}}{7}$
C) $\frac{\sqrt{7}}{3}$
D) $\frac{\sqrt{11}}{3}$
E) $\frac{\sqrt{97}}{12}$

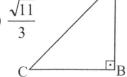

4) $\angle B=90^{\circ}$, AD=20, AB=12, BC=5. What is the value of DC?

A) 3
B) 4
C) 7
D) 9
E) 11

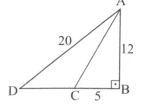

5) AE=7, EC=5, BC=4. What is the value of AB?

A) $\sqrt{10}$
B) $\sqrt{12}$
C) $\sqrt{20}$
D) $\sqrt{25}$
E) $\sqrt{58}$

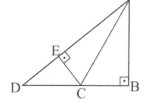

6) $\angle B=90^{\circ}$, AB=5, BC=12. What is the value of AC?

A) 17
B) 16
C) 15
D) 14
E) 13

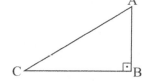

7) $\angle B=90^{\circ}$, AB=4x, BC=8x. What is the area of the triangle ABC?

A) 10x
B) $16x^2$
C) $2x\sqrt{10}$
D) $2x\sqrt{10}+8x$
E) $2\sqrt{10x}+8x$

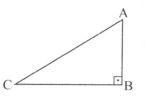

8) AB=7, BD=5, DC=3, $\angle ADC=90^{\circ}$. What is the value of AC?

A) $\sqrt{23}$
B) $2\sqrt{3}$
C) $3\sqrt{2}$
D) $\sqrt{33}$
E) $2\sqrt{6}$

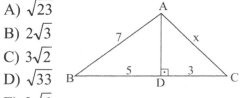

9) $\angle ADC=90^o$, AB=7, AD=5, AC=8. What is the value of BD?

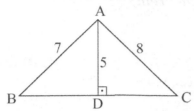

A) $\dfrac{2\sqrt{6}}{1}$ B) $\dfrac{2\sqrt{5}}{\sqrt{11}}$ C) $\dfrac{2\sqrt{5}}{\sqrt{33}}$

D) $\dfrac{3\sqrt{5}}{\sqrt{11}}$ E) $\dfrac{4\sqrt{5}}{\sqrt{33}}$

10) $\angle A=\angle D=90^o$, BD=6, DC=9. What is the ratio of the area of triangle ABD and the area of triangle ADC?

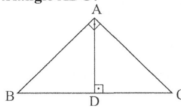

A) $\dfrac{2}{\sqrt{10}}$ B) $\dfrac{2}{9}$ C) $\dfrac{2}{3}$

D) $\dfrac{\sqrt{5}}{\sqrt{13}}$ E) $\dfrac{2}{13}$

11) $\angle A=\angle D=90^o$, BD=4x, DC=5x, What is the value of AD?

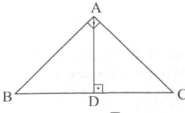

A) $2x\sqrt{5}$ B) $\dfrac{x\sqrt{3}}{2}$ C) $\dfrac{2x}{\sqrt{3}}$

D) $\dfrac{\sqrt{5}}{2}$ E) $\dfrac{\sqrt{5}}{3}$

12) $\angle B=90^o$, AB=2a, BC=5a. What is the perimeter of triangle ABC?

A) $4a+\sqrt{17}$

B) $7a+a\sqrt{29}$

C) $5a+a\sqrt{17}$

D) $6a+\sqrt{17}$

E) $6a+a\sqrt{17}$

13) $\angle B=90^o$, AC=8x, and AB=5x. What is the value of BC?

A) $\dfrac{3x}{3+\sqrt{3}}$

B) $\dfrac{x\sqrt{39}}{1}$

C) $\dfrac{4}{4+4\sqrt{3}}$

D) $\dfrac{5}{2+\sqrt{3}}$ E) $\dfrac{3x}{2+\sqrt{3}}$

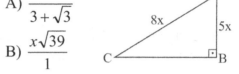

14) $\angle B=90^o$, AB=4, BC=8, what is the area of the triangle ABC?

A) 5 B) 15

C) 32 D) 18

E) 16

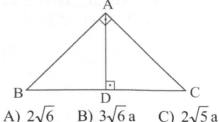

15) $\angle A=\angle D=90^o$, BD=5a, DC=7a, What is the value of AD?

A) $2\sqrt{6}$ B) $3\sqrt{6}\,a$ C) $2\sqrt{5}\,a$

D) $a\,2\sqrt{6}$ E) $a\sqrt{35}$

TEST 23
(Special Right Triangle)

1) ∠B=90°, AB=BC=8. What is the value of AC?

A) $5\sqrt{3}$
B) $8\sqrt{2}$
C) $5\sqrt{4}$
D) 6
E) 7

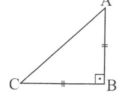

2) ∠B=90°, ∠A=∠C=45°, AC=$12\sqrt{2}$. What is the value of AB+BC?

A) 9
B) 10
C) 11
D) 12
E) 24

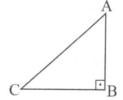

3) ∠B=90°, AC=8, ∠A=∠C=45°, What is the area of triangle ABC?

A) 49
B) 16
C) 32
D) 40
E) 36

4) ∠B=90°, AB=BC=4x. What is the perimeter of triangle ABC?

A) $8 + 4x\sqrt{2}$
B) $3x + 4x\sqrt{3}$
C) $8x + 4x\sqrt{2}$
D) $\dfrac{3 + \sqrt{3}}{3}$
E) $\dfrac{2 + \sqrt{2}}{2}$

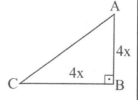

5) ∠B=90°, ∠A=∠C=45°. The area of the triangle ABC is 6cm². What is the perimeter of triangle ABC?

A) $6\sqrt{5}$
B) $2\sqrt{5} + 2\sqrt{10}$
C) $2\sqrt{6} + 4\sqrt{3}$
D) $6 + 2\sqrt{5}$
E) $2\sqrt{10} + 8$

6) ∠A=90°, ∠B=∠C=45°, BC=6cm, $\dfrac{(AB + AC)}{BC} = ?$

A) $\sqrt{2}$
B) $\sqrt{3}$
C) $2\sqrt{2}$
D) $3\sqrt{3}$
E) 4

7) ∠A=60°, ∠B=90°, ∠C=30°, AC=4cm, $\dfrac{BC}{AB} = ?$

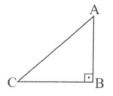

A) 2
B) 3
C) $2\sqrt{2}$
D) $3\sqrt{3}$
E) $\sqrt{3}$

8) ∠A=60°, ∠B=90°, AB=6cm. What is the area of triangle ABC?

A) $32\sqrt{3}$
B) 32
C) 16
D) $18\sqrt{3}$
E) 24

9) ∠A=60°, ∠B=90°, AC=4x. What is the area of triangle ABC?

A) $9x^2$

B) $\dfrac{9\sqrt{3}}{2}$

C) $\dfrac{6x^2}{5}$

D) $\dfrac{9x\sqrt{3}}{2}$

E) $2x^2\sqrt{3}$

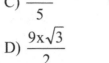

12) ∠C=90°, ∠BAC=45°, ∠CAD=30°, AD=10. What is the value of AB?

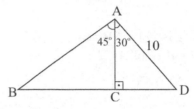

A) 6   B) $5\sqrt{6}$ C) $3\sqrt{2}$

D) $3\sqrt{3}$ E) $3\sqrt{6}$

10) ∠B=90°, ∠D=30°, DC=AC=8. What is the value of BC?

A) 2

B) $2\sqrt{3}$

C) 3

D) $3\sqrt{3}$

E) 4

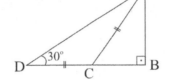

13) ∠A=∠D=90°, AB=6, AC=8, and BD=4. What is the value of DC?

A) 6

B) 7

C) 8

D) 9

E) 10

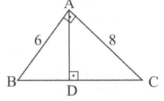

11) ∠B=90°, ∠C=15°, ∠DAB=30°, AB=5. What is the value of AD?

A) 12

B) 9

C) $6\sqrt{3}$

D) $5\sqrt{2}$

E) $6\sqrt{5}$

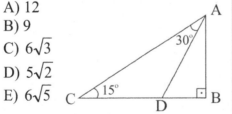

14) ∠B=90°, AC=13, BC=5, AD=7. What is the value of BD?

A) 9

B) 8

C) 7

D) 6

E) 5

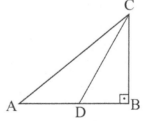

15) ∠B=90°, AB=4x, BC=4y. What is the value of AC=?

A) $3\sqrt{x^2 + y^2}$

B) $9x^2+9y^2$

C) $9\sqrt{x + y}$

D) $4\sqrt{x^2 + y^2}$

E) 3x+3y

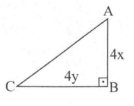

TEST 24
(Vectors)

1) If $\vec{A} = (3i + 5j)$ and $\vec{B} = (2i + 2j)$ the result vector of $3\vec{A} + 2\vec{B}$ equals.
   A) 13i+19j   B) 18i+21j
   C) 17i+17j   D) 8i+8j
   E) 20i+21j

2) $\vec{A} = (7, 6)$, $\vec{B} = (8, 2)$. What is the magnitude of $\vec{A} + \vec{B}$.
   A) 3   B) 4   C) 5
   D) (8, 15)   E) (15, 8)

3) Let it i, j and k be unit vectors in the x, y and z directions. Suppose that $\vec{A} = 3i - 4j + 4k$. what is the magnitude of the vector A?
   A) 11   B) $\sqrt{41}$ C) 21
   D) $\sqrt{29}$ E) $\sqrt{39}$

4) Let it i, j and k be unit vectors in the x, y and z directions. Suppose that $\vec{A} = 5i - 3j + 4k$. What is the magnitude of the vector A?
   A) 12   B) $5\sqrt{2}$ C) 24
   D) $\sqrt{24}$ E) $\sqrt{29}$

5) Relative to the origin point A has a position vector 6i+8j and B has position vector 4i–4j. What is $\overrightarrow{AB}$?
   A) 6i+8j   B) 6i–4j
   C) 2i+12j   D) 8i+6j
   E) 10i+8j

6) Let it i and j be unit vectors in the x andy directions respectively. Suppose that A=9i–12j. What is the magnitude of the vector A?
   A) 15   B) 13   C) 12
   D) 11   E) 10

7) Let $\vec{A} = (-7, 5)$ and $\vec{B} = (8, 6)$. What is the component form of the sum $\vec{A} + \vec{B}$.
   A) (–4, 9)   B) (–13, 9)
   C) (1, 11)   D) (–1, 9)
   E) (3, 4)

8) What is the magnitude of the vector $\vec{A} = (4, 6)$?
   A) 24   B) $\sqrt{24}$ C) 34
   D) $2\sqrt{13}$ E) 6

9) Multiply the vector $\vec{A} = (8; 3)$ by the scalar 4.
   A) (18; 8)   B) (32; 12)
   C) (36; 16)   D) (20; 36)
   E) (45; 20)

10) Add the vectors $\vec{A} = (2;\ 3;\ 4)$ and $\vec{B} = (5;\ 6;\ 7)$.

A) $(5;\ 7;\ 9)$
B) $(5;\ 7;\ 8)$
C) $(7;\ 9;\ 11)$
D) $(6;\ 7;\ 10)$
E) $(9;\ 8;\ 12)$

11) What is the magnitude of the vector $\vec{B} = (3;\ -4;\ -5)$?

A) 29 B) $5\sqrt{2}$ C) 26
D) $\sqrt{26}$ E) 6

12) $\vec{A} = (1;\ 2;\ 3)$, $\vec{B} = (1;\ 3;\ 4)$ and $\vec{C} = 2\vec{A} - 3\vec{B}$. What is the magnitude of $\vec{C}$?

A) $\sqrt{32}$ B) $\sqrt{42}$ C) $\sqrt{52}$
D) $\sqrt{62}$ E) $\sqrt{72}$

13) If $\vec{A} = (7;\ 5)$ and $\vec{B} = (-5;\ -3)$. What is the $\vec{A} + \vec{B}$?

A) $(10;\ 2)$
B) $(10;\ -2)$
C) $(2;\ 2)$
D) $(-2;\ -2)$
E) $(3;\ 6)$

14) What is $\vec{A} + \vec{B}$?

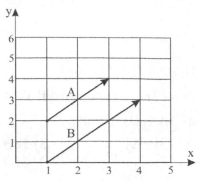

A) $(3;\ 3)$ B) $(3;\ 5)$ C) $(5;\ 5)$
D) $(4;\ 4)$ E) $(6;\ 5)$

15) What is $\vec{A} + 2\vec{B} + \vec{C}$?

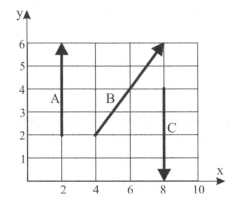

A) $(4;\ 8)$ B) $(7;\ 7)$ C) $(6;\ 8)$
D) $(8;\ 6)$ E) $(12;\ 4)$

TEST 25
(Equations of Circle)

1) Circle with center (0, 0), radius 6. What is the formula?

A) $x^2+y^2=7$
B) $x^2+y^2=14$
C) $x^2+y^2=36$
D) $x^2+y^2=\sqrt{7}$
E) $x^2+y^2=\sqrt{14}$

2) Circle with center (4, –7), radius 5. What is the formula?

A) $(x-2)^2+(y+6)^2=8$
B) $(x-4)^2+(y-7)^2=16$
C) $(x+4)^2+(y+7)^2=25$
D) $(x-4)^2+(y+7)^2=25$
E) $x^2+y^2=16$

3) $x^2+y^2+14x+16y+14=0$. What is the coordinate of the center of the circle?

A) (8, 10)
B) (–8, 10)
C) (–4, –5)
D) (4, 5)
E) (-7, -8)

4) $3x^2+3y^2+15x-12y+18=0$. What is the coordinate of the center of the circle?

A) $\left(2, \dfrac{5}{2}\right)$ B) $\left(-2, \dfrac{5}{2}\right)$

C) $\left(-\dfrac{5}{2}, -2\right)$ D) $\left(2, -\dfrac{5}{2}\right)$

E) (–2, 4)

5) What is the equation for the circle shown below if it is shifted five units to the right and three units up?

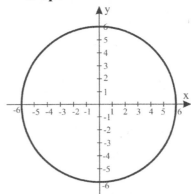

A) $(x-5)^2+(y-3)^2=36$
B) $(x+5)^2+(y-3)^2=36$
C) $(x-2)^2+(y+3)^2=6$
D) $(x+2)^2+(y-3)^2=36$
E) $(x+2)^2+(y+3)^2=18$

6) $(x-8)^2+(y-5)^2=49$. What is the center coordinates of the circle?

A) (–6, 5)   B) (–6, –5)

C) (8, 5)   D) (5, 6)

E) (–5, –6)

7) $(x-6)^2+(y-8)^2=100$. What is the radius of the circle?

A) 3   B) 4   C) 5
D) 10   E) 25

8) What is the equation of the circle in general form?

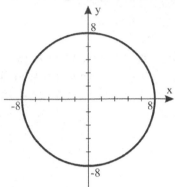

A) $x^2+y^2=64$ B) $x^2+y^2=36$
C) $x^2+y^2=8$ D) $x^2+y^2=\sqrt{8}$
E) $x^2+y^2+64=0$

9) A circle has a center $(4, -5)$ and the point $(-2, -9)$ lies on the circumference of the circle. What is the equation of the circle in standard form?
A) $(x-4)^2+(y-5)^2=26$
B) $(x-4)^2+(y+5)^2=52$
C) $(x-4)^2+(y+5)^2=26$
D) $(x-3)^2+(y+5)^2=52$
E) $(x-4)^2+(y+6)^2=26$

10) A circle has a center $(-8, 12)$ and the point $(5, -2)$ lies on the circumference of the circle. What is the equation of the circle in standard form?
A) $(x+8)^2+(y-12)^2=\sqrt{313}$
B) $(x+8)^2+(y+12)^2=\sqrt{313}$
C) $(x-8)^2+(y+12)^2=313$
D) $(x-8)^2+(y-10)^2=313$
E) $(x+8)^2+(y-12)^2=365$

11) What is the center of circle for $(x-6)^2+(y+2)^2=64$?
A) $(-6, -2)$ B) $(6, -3)$
C) $(2, -6)$ D) $(2, 6)$
E) $(6, -2)$

12) What is the radius of the circle for $(x+5)^2+(y-12)^2=169$?
A) 13   B) 12   C) 14
D) 15   E) 16

13) What is the center of the circle $x^2+y^2+14x-22y+52=0$?
A) $(16, -24)$ B) $(16, -12)$
C) $(8, -12)$ D) $(-7, 11)$
E) $(-8, -12)$

14) What is the radius of circle $x^2+y^2-7x+13y-20=0$?
A) $\sqrt{298}$ B) $2\sqrt{298}$
C) $\dfrac{\sqrt{298}}{2}$ D) $\dfrac{\sqrt{198}}{2}$
E) $\dfrac{\sqrt{198}}{3}$

15) $x^2+y^2=225$. What is the value of r?
A) 25
B) 18
C) 16
D) 15
E) 12

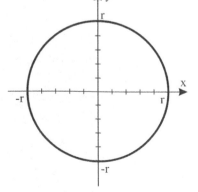

TEST 26

(Angle measures in Polygon)

1) How many sides does a polygon have if the sum of its interior angle is 540°?

A) 8   B) 7   C) 6
D) 5   E) 4

2) How many sides does a polygon have if the sum of its interior angle is 1440°?

A) 12   B) 11   C) 10
D) 8   E) 8

3) What is the size of one interior angle of a regular eighteen-side polygon?

A) 170   B) 160   C) 150
D) 140   E) 130

4) Each of the interior angles of a regular polygon is 160°. How many sides does the polygon have?

A) 20   B) 18   C) 16
D) 14   E) 12

5) What is the sum of the interior angles of a regular fourteen–sided polygon?

A) 1800   B) 1900   C) 2000
D) 2160   E) 2260

6) The diagram is the Pentagon. $\angle A=60°$, $\angle B=110°$, $\angle C=114°$, and $\angle D=20°$. What is the value of x?

A) 120
B) 124
C) 130
D) 136
E) 104

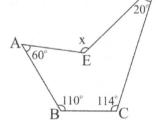

7) What is the measure of each interior angle in a regular hexagon?

A) 45   B) 60   C) 75
D) 100   E) 120

8) if a regular polygon with an exterior angle is 30°, how many sides does the polygon have?

A) 10   B) 11   C) 12
D) 13   E) 14

9) The sum of the measures of the interior angles of a dodecagon (side is 12)?

A) 1160   B) 1060   C) 1888
D) 1800   E) 2160

10) What is the value of α?

A) 45
B) 50
C) 55
D) 60
E) 70

A
110°
D 90°
α B
115°
C

11) What is the value of x?

A) 91
B) 101
C) 111
D) 121
E) 124

D
E 118°
115°
A 120°
96° C
x°
B

Use the following figure for questions 12, 13, 14, and 15.

AB=BC=DC=DE=EF=FA=10cm

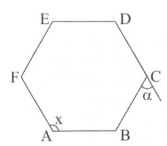

12) What is the value of α?

A) 30
B) 36
C) 40
D) 60
E) 70

13) What is the value of x?

A) 110
B) 115
C) 120
D) 124
E) 125

14) What is the perimeter of the hexagon ABCDEF?

A) 24   B) 30   C) 36
D) 40   E) 60

15) Find the area of the hexagon ABCDEF?

A) 150   B) $150\sqrt{2}$

C) $150\sqrt{3}$ D) 160

E) $160\sqrt{3}$

TEST 27
(Tangents to Circle)

1) $\overrightarrow{AB}$ is tangent to circle M at A. $\overleftrightarrow{BC}$ is tangent to circle M at C. What is the value of 3x?

A) 8
B) 7
C) 6
D) 5
E) 12

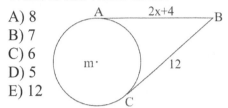

5) AB=4x+8, BC=3x+16. What is the value of x?

A) 10
B) 9
C) 8
D) 7
E) 6

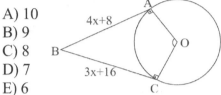

2) AB=x^2-7, BC=42. What is the value of x?

A) 7
B) –6
C) 6
D) 12
E) –12

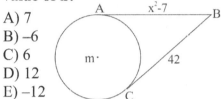

6) AB=x^2–4, BC=21. What is the value of x?

A) ±6
B) 7
C) ±5
D) 8
E) 9

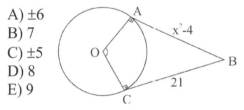

3) AB=15, BC=x. What is the value of 2x?

A) 22
B) 18
C) 15
D) 14
E) 30

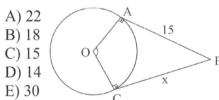

7) AB=12, AD=9, D is the center of the circle. What is the value of BC?

A) 1
B) 2
C) 3
D) 4
E) 6

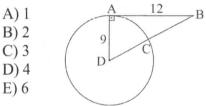

4) AB=5x, BC=25. What is the value of 3x?

A) 18
B) 17
C) 12
D) 15
E) 10

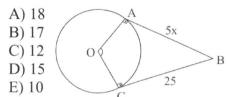

8) AD=r=12, BC=8. What is the value of AB?

A) 14
B) 13
C) 12
D) 11
E) 16

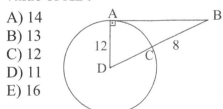

9) O is the center of the circle. AB=26, BC=10. What is the value of r?

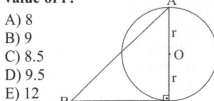

A) 8
B) 9
C) 8.5
D) 9.5
E) 12

10) O is the center of the circle. CK=8cm. What is the value of DK?

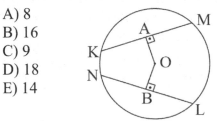

A) 8
B) 3
C) 4
D) 5
E) 6

11) KM=16 cm, AO=OB. What is the value of NL?

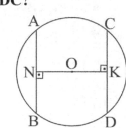

A) 8
B) 16
C) 9
D) 18
E) 14

12) O is the center of the circle. AB=13cm, NO=OK. What is the value of DC?

A) 16
B) 14
C) 12
D) 13
E) 6.5

13) O is the center of the circle. ∠A=90°, AB=24, AO=10. What is the value of BK?

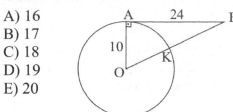

A) 16
B) 17
C) 18
D) 19
E) 20

14) ∠A=90°, AO=3 cm, AB=4cm, $\dfrac{BK}{OK} = ?$

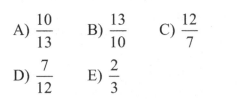

A) $\dfrac{10}{13}$　　B) $\dfrac{13}{10}$　　C) $\dfrac{12}{7}$

D) $\dfrac{7}{12}$　　E) $\dfrac{2}{3}$

15) ∠A=90°, OC=5, BC=7, O is the center of the circle. What is the value of AB?

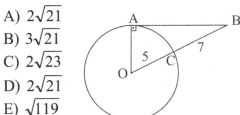

A) $2\sqrt{21}$
B) $3\sqrt{21}$
C) $2\sqrt{23}$
D) $2\sqrt{21}$
E) $\sqrt{119}$

TEST 28
(Inscribed Angles)

1) O is the center of the circle.

$\overset{\frown}{AB}=84°$. What is the value of α?

A) 42
B) 84
C) 50
D) 40
E) 30

2) ∠D=122°. What is the value of ∠$\overset{\frown}{ABC}$?

A) 120
B) 180
C) 200
D) 240
E) 244

3) ∠A=54°. What is the value of ∠x?

A) 27
B) 54
C) 44
D) 66
E) 88

4) ∠$\overset{\frown}{ABC}$=260°. What is the value of α?

A) 220
B) 200
C) 130
D) 160
E) 110

5) What is the value of ∠α?

A) 140
B) 70
C) 160
D) 170
E) 60

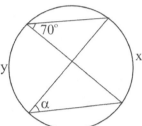

6) ∠D=42°, ∠B=38°, ∠C=y, ∠A=x. What is the value of 2x+3y?

A) 180
B) 188
C) 190
D) 198
E) 208

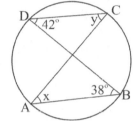

7) ∠$\overset{\frown}{AB}$=112°, ∠DC=72°. What is the value of α?

A) 100
B) 95
C) 90
D) 85
E) 92

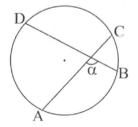

8) $\overset{\frown}{AD}$=178°, $\overset{\frown}{BD}$=48°. What is the value of ∠BCD?

A) 60
B) 65
C) 70
D) 75
E) 80

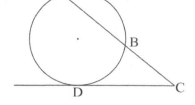

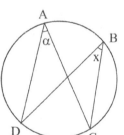

9) $\angle \overset{\frown}{AC}=240^{\circ}$ and $\angle B=3x$. What is the value of x?

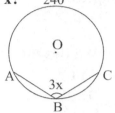

A) 21
B) 42
C) 43
D) 44
E) 80

13) $\angle \overset{\frown}{AB}=138^{\circ}$, $\angle \overset{\frown}{DC}=2x$, and $\angle AKC=85^{\circ}$. What is the value of x?

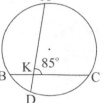

A) 70
B) 80
C) 85
D) 90
E) 95

10) $\angle \overset{\frown}{ADC}=128^{\circ}$. What is the value of α?

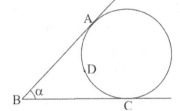

A) 50
B) 58
C) 52
D) 40
E) 36

14) $\angle \overset{\frown}{AB}=4x$, $\angle \overset{\frown}{DC}=3x$, and $\angle AOB=63^{\circ}$. What is the value of x?

A) $\dfrac{88}{7}$ B) $\dfrac{88}{5}$

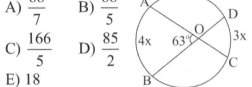

C) $\dfrac{166}{5}$ D) $\dfrac{85}{2}$

E) 18

11) $\angle \overset{\frown}{AE}=88^{\circ}$, $\angle \overset{\frown}{BD}=28^{\circ}$. What is the value of $\angle C$?

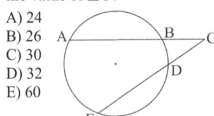

A) 24
B) 26
C) 30
D) 32
E) 60

15) $\angle A=10^{\circ}$,

$\angle \overset{\frown}{BC}=4x^{\circ}$,

$\angle \overset{\frown}{DE}=6x^{\circ}$,

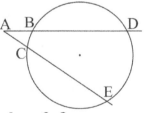

What is the value of x?

A) 54   B) 50   C) 48
D) 44   E) 36

12) What is the value of 4x?

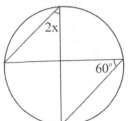

A) 160
B) 145
C) 140
D) 120
E) 125

TEST 29

(Segment Length in Circle)

1) **Chords $\overline{AB}$ and $\overline{DC}$ intersect inside the circle. What is the value of the value of DC?**

A) 11
B) 12
C) 13
D) 14
E) 15

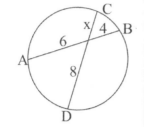

5) **AD=9, BD=4, DC=8. What is the value of ED?**

A) $\dfrac{46}{3}$
B) $\dfrac{56}{3}$
C) 21
D) 18
E) 17

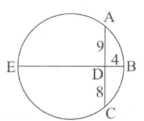

2) **BC=6, BA=12, CD=8. What is the value of DE?**

A) 2
B) 3
C) 4
D) 6
E) 5.5

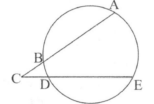

6) **AB=8, BC=4. What is the value of BD?**

A) 12
B) 11
C) 10
D) 14
E) 16

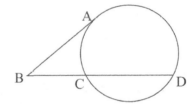

3) **What is the value of CE?**

A) 11
B) 12
C) 13
D) 14
E) 5

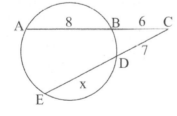

7) **BC=2x, CE=6x, DC=15, AC=8. What is the value of x?**

A) $2\sqrt{3}$
B) $3\sqrt{3}$
C) $2\sqrt{5}$
D) $\sqrt{10}$
E) $3\sqrt{7}$

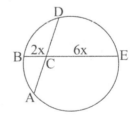

4) **AB=7, BC=6. What is the value of x?**

A) $\sqrt{44}$
B) $\sqrt{50}$
C) $\sqrt{55}$
D) $\sqrt{78}$
E) 7

8) **What is the value of x?**

A) 2
B) 3
C) 4
D) 6
E) 7

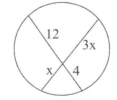

9) AD=AE=4, BD=4x, EC=8. What is the value of x?

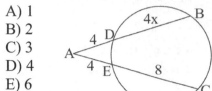

A) 1
B) 2
C) 3
D) 4
E) 6

13) What is the value of AC?

A) 5
B) 6
C) 10
D) $2\sqrt{5}$
E) $2\sqrt{6}$

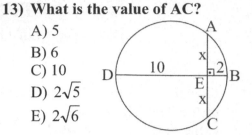

10) What is the value of x?

A) $3\sqrt{3}$
B) $2\sqrt{3}$
C) $3\sqrt{3}$
D) $3\sqrt{5}$
E) $\sqrt{5}$

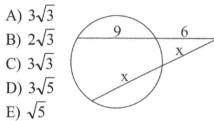

14) BC=4, DC=8. What is the value of AB?

A) $\sqrt{3}$
B) $\sqrt{6}$
C) $2\sqrt{2}$
D) $2\sqrt{3}$
E) $4\sqrt{3}$

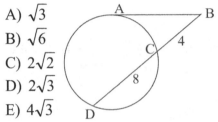

11) O is the center of the circle. AB=10, BC=6. What is the value of r?

A) 2
B) 3
C) 4
D) 6
E) $\dfrac{16}{3}$

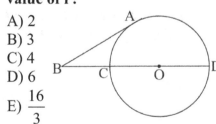

15) CB=4, BA=8, CD=4. What is the value of DE?

A) 6
B) 8
C) 5
D) 9
E) $\dfrac{27}{4}$

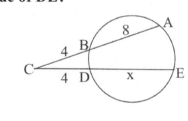

12) BC=6, CO=8. What is the value of AB?

A) $\sqrt{10}$
B) $4\sqrt{6}$
C) $3\sqrt{10}$
D) $3\sqrt{5}$
E) $3\sqrt{6}$

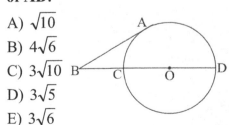

TEST 30
(Circumference and Arc Length)

1) α=45°, r=10cm. What is the length of arc AB?

A) π
B) 2π
C) $\frac{3\pi}{2}$
D) 4π
E) $\frac{5\pi}{2}$

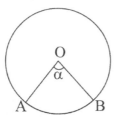

2) α=130°, r=8 cm. What is the length of arc AB?

A) $\frac{4\pi}{3}$
B) $\frac{2\pi}{3}$
C) $\frac{3\pi}{2}$
D) $\frac{52\pi}{9}$
E) 3π

3) What is the circumference of a circle with radius 9 inch?

A) 20π   B) 18π   C) 12π
D) 11π   E) 10π

4) What is the radius of a circle with circumference 18π?

A) 2   B) 3   C) 4
D) 5   E) 9

5) ∠BOC=33° and AB=20 cm. What is the length of each arc BC?

A) $\frac{10\pi}{3}$ B) $\frac{4\pi}{3}$
C) $\frac{11\pi}{6}$ D) $\frac{5\pi}{7}$
E) 2π

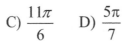

6) What is the diameter of a circle with the circumference $10\sqrt{2}\,\pi$?

A) $\sqrt{3}$ B) $10\sqrt{2}$ C) $3\sqrt{3}$
D) $4\sqrt{3}$ E) $8\sqrt{3}$

7) O is the center of the circle. ∠AOB=144°, BO=8cm. What is the length of arc $\overset{\frown}{ACD}$ = ?

A) $\frac{8\pi}{5}$ B) $\frac{25\pi}{9}$
C) $\frac{35\pi}{7}$ D) $\frac{35\pi}{8}$
E) $\frac{32\pi}{5}$

8) AO=18cm, ∠AOB=30°, $\overset{\frown}{AB}$ = ?

A) $\frac{2\pi}{3}$ B) $\frac{3\pi}{2}$
C) $\frac{4\pi}{3}$ D) $\frac{3\pi}{4}$ E) 3π

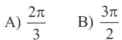

9) What is the circumference of a circle with diameter $\sqrt{60}cm.$?

A) 2π B) 22π C) $2\pi\sqrt{15}$

D) $11\pi\sqrt{2}$ E) $2\sqrt{11}\pi$

13) AO=$2\sqrt{3}$, $\angle AOB=45^\circ$. What is the length of $\overset{\frown}{AB}$?

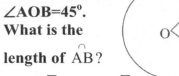

A) $\dfrac{2\sqrt{3}\pi}{9}$ B) $\dfrac{\pi\sqrt{3}}{2}$

C) $\dfrac{2\sqrt{3}}{9}$ D) $\dfrac{3\sqrt{2}\pi}{9}$ E) $\dfrac{4\sqrt{2}\pi}{9}$

10) The circle radius is 10cm. What is the area of a circle?

A) 95π B) 100π C) 105π

D) 100 E) 115π

14) The radius of a circle is 20. What is the length of an arc of the circle intercepted by a central angle measuring 20°?

A) $\dfrac{9\pi}{2}$ B) $\dfrac{9\pi}{7}$ C) $\dfrac{9\pi}{5}$

D) $\dfrac{7\pi}{3}$ E) $\dfrac{20\pi}{9}$

11) O is the center of the circle. $\angle AOB=135^\circ$, $\overline{AB}=5x+60^\circ$, What is the value of x?

A) 5
B) 10
C) 15
D) 20
E) 25

15) What is the circumference of a circle with a diameter $\sqrt{90}\ cm.$?

A) $3\sqrt{10}\pi$ B) $2\sqrt{10}\pi$

C) $\sqrt{10}\pi$ D) $2\pi\sqrt{10}$

E) $2\pi\sqrt{15}$

12) The radius of a circle is 16. What is the length of an arc of the circle intercepted by a central angle measuring 120°?

A) $\dfrac{11\pi}{3}$ B) $\dfrac{32\pi}{3}$ C) $\dfrac{24\pi}{5}$

D) $\dfrac{256\pi}{3}$ E) $\dfrac{26\pi}{3}$

TEST 31
(Areas of Circles and Sectors)

1) r=1.3cm. What is the area of the circle?

A) 1.69π
B) 16.9π
C) 13π
D) 26π
E) 144π

2) A=225π. What is the radius of the circle?

A) 10
B) 15
C) 25
D) 14
E) 28

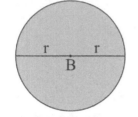

3) A=196π. What is the diameter of the circle?

A) 36
B) 35
C) 34
D) 28
E) 17π

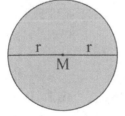

4) ∠AOB=75°, BO=6. What is the area of the sector shown at the right?

A) $\dfrac{12\pi}{5}$

B) $\dfrac{13\pi}{5}$

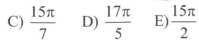

C) $\dfrac{15\pi}{7}$ D) $\dfrac{17\pi}{5}$ E) $\dfrac{15\pi}{2}$

5) ∠AOB=72°, r=10cm. What is the area of the sector shown at the right?

A) 27π
B) 26π
C) 25π
D) 24π
E) 20π

6) AO=6cm, $\angle \overline{ACB}=130^o$. What is the area of the shaded region?

A) 14π
B) 18π
C) 20π
D) 13π
E) 56π

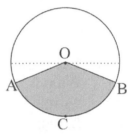

7) $AB=2\sqrt{13}\,cm$, What is the area of the circle?

A) 12π
B) 10π
C) 13π
D) 6π
E) $2\sqrt{3}\,\pi$

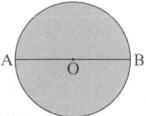

8) AO=8cm, AO=OB=AB. What is the area of the shaded region?

A) $8\pi-8\sqrt{3}$
B) $32\pi/3-16\sqrt{3}$
C) $33\pi/3-16\sqrt{3}$
D) $6\pi+9\sqrt{3}$
E) $12\pi-9\sqrt{3}$

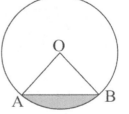

9) AO=6cm, ∠AOB=40°. What is the area of the shaded region?

A) 25π
B) 29π
C) 30π
D) 32π
E) 34π

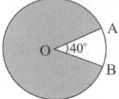

10) AD=10, BC=6. What is the area of the shaded region?

A) 16π
B) 23π
C) 20π
D) 12π
E) 10π

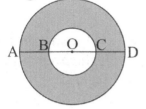

11) The radius of the circle is 10cm. What is the area of the circle?

A) 10π
B) 25π
C) 64π
D) 100π
E) 225π

12) O is the center of the circle. AO=8cm, ∠AOB=100°. What is the area of the shaded region?

A) 6π
B) 7π
C) $\frac{24\pi}{7}$
D) $\frac{24\pi}{5}$
E) $\frac{160\pi}{9}$

13) $AB = 4\sqrt{11}$, $DC = 8\sqrt{7}$. What is the ratio of the area of the shaded circles?

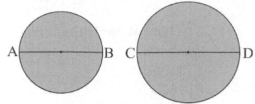

A) $\frac{11}{28}$ B) $\frac{1}{3}$ C) 3

D) $\frac{3}{2}$ E) $\frac{3}{4}$

14) $AB = \sqrt{66}$. What is the area of the shaded region?

A) 33π
B) 22π
C) $\sqrt{11}\pi$
D) $\sqrt{33}\pi$
E) $\frac{33\pi}{4}$

15) A and B are circle center. BC=2cm. What is the area of the shaded region?

A) 12π
B) 24π
C) 48π
D) 50π
E) 64π

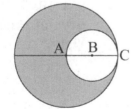

TEST 32
(Surface Area of Prism and Cylinder)

1) What is the surface area of the right prism?

A) 170
B) 200
C) 250
D) 300
E) 472

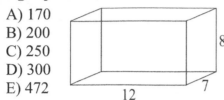

2) What is the surface area of the rectangular prism?

A) 80
B) 90
C) 100
D) 108
E) 180

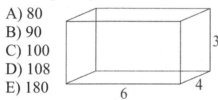

3) What is the surface area of the rectangular prism?

Λ) 376
B) 186
C) 176
D) 166
E) 156

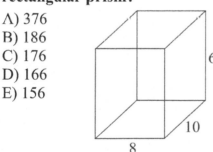

4) What is the surface area of the the rectangular prism with the sides of lengths 3, 4, and 5cm?

A) 90   B) 94   C) 96
D) 98   E) 104

5) What is the surface area of a rectangular prism if the base is square with edge length 8cm and height 3cm?

A) 124
B) 144
C) 164
D) 184
E) 224

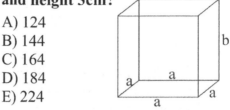

6) What is the surface of a right rectangular prism with a height of 7cm, a length of 4cm and width of 6cm?

A) 148
B) 168
C) 178
D) 188
E) 208

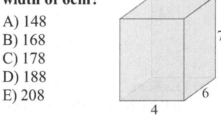

7) FC=12, DF=9, AD=13cm. What is the surface area of the triangular prism?

A) 576
B) 546
C) 476
D) 466
E) 356

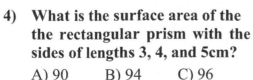

8) <E=<F=90°, EA=5, BE=12, BC=8cm. What is the surface area of the triangular prism?

A) 200
B) 220
C) 300
D) 360
E) 380

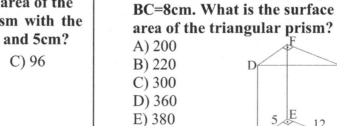

9) $\dfrac{1}{a}+\dfrac{1}{b}+\dfrac{1}{c}=3$ and $\upsilon=144cm^3$.

What is the surface area of rectangular prism?

A) 800
B) 824
C) 844
D) 846
E) 864

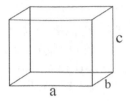

13) AB=6x, BC=2x. What is the surface area of the cylinder?

A) 30π
B) $30\pi x^2$
C) $30\pi x$
D) 36π
E) $36\pi x^2$

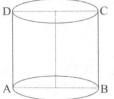

10) KL=5cm, LD=4cm. What is the surface area of the right cylinder?

A) 40π
B) 50π
C) 62π
D) 72π
E) 84π

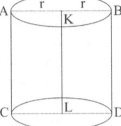

14) ABCD is a cylinder. $\dfrac{r}{h}=\dfrac{1}{3}$.

What is the surface area of the cylinder?

A) $3\pi r^2$
B) $4\pi r^2$
C) $8\pi r^2$
D) 10π
E) $10\pi r^2$

11) AB=6cm, r=3cm. What is the surface area of the cylinder?

A) 54π
B) 54
C) 44π
D) 44
E) 34π

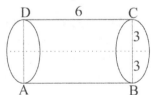

15) AB=3^{2x}, BC=3^x. What is the surface area of the cylinder?

A) $3^{3x}\pi+2\cdot3^{4x}\pi$

B) $\dfrac{3^{4x}\cdot\pi}{2}+3^{3x}\pi$

C) $3^{3x}\pi+3^{4x}$

D) $\dfrac{3^{4x}\cdot\pi}{3}+3^{3x}+\pi$

E) $3^{3x}\pi+4\cdot3^{2x}\pi$

12) BC=11cm, AB=12cm. What is the surface area of the cylinder?

A) 200
B) 214π
C) 206π
D) 204π
E) 224

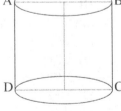

TEST 33
(Surface Area of Pyramids and Cones)

1) What is the surface area of the triangular pyramid if the area of its base is 16cm² and each of its literal faces has area 9cm²?

A) 43 B) 44 C) 46
D) 47 E) 48

2) What is the base area of a square pyramid whose base has a side length of 12cm?

A) 148 B) 144 C) 143
D) 140 E) 121

3) The base area of a square pyramid is 225cm². What is the length of an edge of the base of the pyramid?

A) 12 B) 13 C) 14
D) 15 E) 16

4) The square pyramid with base length 16 in and height 6cm. What is the surface area of the square pyramid?

A) 126
B) 132
C) 220
D) 256
E) 264

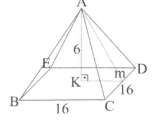

5) What is the surface area of the pyramid?

A) 426
B) 526
C) 576
D) 580
E) 600

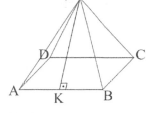

6) EK=8, AB=6. What is the surface area of the regular pyramid?

A) 96
B) 102
C) 122
D) 130
E) 132

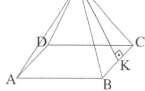

7) AB=4, EK=5. AB=BC. What is the surface area of the pyramid?

A) 48
B) 50
C) 54
D) 52
E) 56

8) AB=BC=9, EK=12. What is the surface area of the pyramid?

A) 280
B) 282
C) 297
D) 300
E) 312

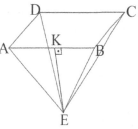

9) What is the surface area of the cone?

A) 48π
B) 49π
C) 50π
D) 51π
E) 60π

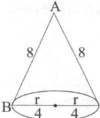

13) AK=16, KC=12. What is the surface area of the right cone?

A) 360π
B) 384π
C) 390π
D) 400π
E) 420π

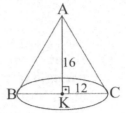

10) AC=13, BC=10cm. What is the surface area of the right cone?

A) 90
B) 80π
C) 90π
D) 100π
E) 121π

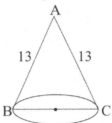

14) KC=4, AK=6. What is the surface area of the right cone?

A) 140.88
B) 130.88
C) 120.88
D) 110.88
E) 98.88

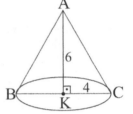

11) AB=16, AC=12. What is the surface area of the right cone?

A) 132π
B) 132
C) 144π
D) 144
E) 256π

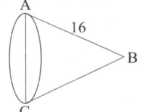

15) DC=10, AD=12. What is the slant height of the right cone?

A) $\sqrt{61}$
B) $2\sqrt{61}$
C) $\sqrt{71}$
D) $2\sqrt{71}$
E) 18

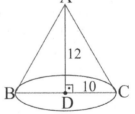

12) AB=24cm, CK=5cm. What is the slant height of the right cone?

A) 10
B) 11
C) 12
D) 13
E) 14

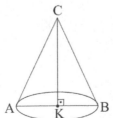

TEST 34

(Volume of Prisms and Cylinders)

1) a=6cm. What is the volume of the prisms?

    A) 36
    B) 108
    C) 124
    D) 216
    E) 230

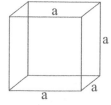

2) What is the volume of the prisms?

    A) 430
    B) 480
    C) 490
    D) 512
    E) 480π

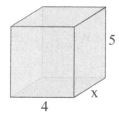

3) The volume of the prism is 240cm³. What is the value of x?

    A) 12
    B) 13
    C) 14
    D) 15
    E) 16

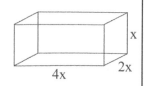

4) What is the volume of a prism where the base area is 36cm² and which is 13cm long?

    A) 458   B) 468   C) 478
    D) 512   E) 578

5) V=64cm³. What is the value of 2x?

    A) 2
    B) 4
    C) 5
    D) 6
    E) 7

6) What is the volume of the right prisms?

    A) 123
    B) 243
    C) 333
    D) 343
    E) 363

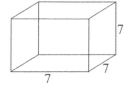

7) What is the volume of the right prism?

    A) 90
    B) 120
    C) 220
    D) 320
    E) 420

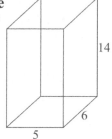

8) What is the ratio of the volume of the first prism and the volume of the second prism below?

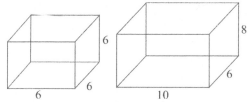

    A) $\frac{9}{22}$ B) $\frac{9}{20}$ C) $\frac{7}{20}$

    D) $\frac{8}{21}$ E) $\frac{10}{21}$

9) r=4cm, h=8cm. What is the volume of the right cylinder?

    A) 100π
    B) 112π
    C) 128π
    D) 130π
    E) 168π

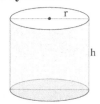

10) r=4cm, h=4cm. What is the volume of the right cylinder?

A) 64π
B) 64
C) 100π
D) 100
E) 32π

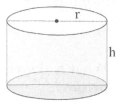

14) AB=8cm, BC=18cm. What is the volume of the oblique cylinder?

A) 1152
B) 1152π
C) 1262π
D) 1262
E) 166π

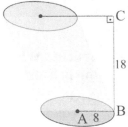

11) AB=4cm, BD=12cm. What is the volume of the right cylinder?

A) 40π
B) 48π
C) 50π
D) 50π
E) 64π

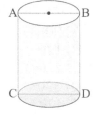

15) AB=20cm, BC=10cm. F=12cm, KF=10cm. What is the ratio of the volume of the first cylinder and the volume of the second cylinder below?

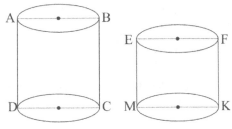

A) $\dfrac{25}{9}$ B) $\dfrac{10}{7}$ C) $\dfrac{11}{3}$

D) $\dfrac{11}{7}$ E) 2

12) r=6cm, AB=10cm. What is the volume of the oblique cylinder?

A) 100π
B) 120π
C) 180π
D) 360π
E) 380π

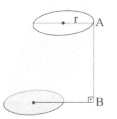

13) AB=3cm, AD=14cm. What is the volume of the right cylinder?

A) 80π
B) 90π
C) 90
D) 120π
E) 126π

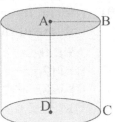

TEST 35

(Volume of Pyramids and Cones)

1) EK=20, AB=12. What is the volume of the pyramid with the square base shown the right?

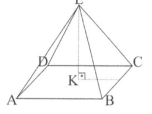

A) 860
B) 960
C) 980
D) 1000
E) 1200

2) AB=BC=14cm, EK=16cm. What is the volume of the pyramid?

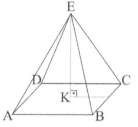

A) 1000
B) 1015
C) 1045
D) 1060
E) 1080

3) ∠B=90°, AB=9, BC−12, h=16. What is the volume of the pyramid?

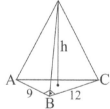

A) 158
B) 168
C) 178
D) 288
E) 208

4) AB=BC=AC=6cm, h=8cm. What is the volume of the pyramid?

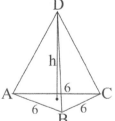

A) $12\sqrt{3}$
B) $14\sqrt{3}$
C) $16\sqrt{3}$
D) $20\sqrt{3}$
E) $24\sqrt{3}$

5) ABCD is square. EK=14cm, AB=12cm. What is the volume of the pyramid?

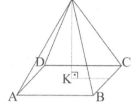

A) 672
B) 675
C) 682
D) 782
E) 800

6) AB=BC=CD=DE=EF=FA=10cm, h=18cm. What is the volume of the pyramid?

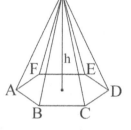

A) $500\sqrt{3}$
B) $600\sqrt{3}$
C) $700\sqrt{3}$
D) $900\sqrt{3}$
E) 1200

7) AB=BC=AC−15cm, h=21cm. What is the volume of the pyramid?

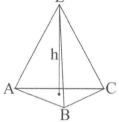

A) $320\sqrt{3}$
B) $340\sqrt{3}$
C) $394\sqrt{3}$
D) 394
E) $396\sqrt{2}$

8) AB=BC=20cm, EK=22cm. What is the volume of the pyramid?

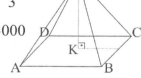

A) $\dfrac{7700}{4}$ B) $\dfrac{8800}{3}$
C) $\dfrac{9400}{3}$ D) 3000
E) 2500

9) ABC is the right circular cone. KC=6cm, AK=10cm. What is the volume of the cone?

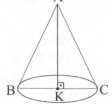

A) 110π
B) 120π
C) 130π
D) 140π
E) 150π

10) r=5cm, h=8cm. What is the volume of the cone?

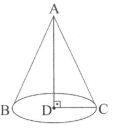

A) $\dfrac{200}{3}$

B) $\dfrac{200\pi}{3}$

C) $\dfrac{400}{3}$

D) $\dfrac{400\pi}{3}$

E) 60π

11) DC=7cm, AD=10cm. What is the volume of the cone?

A) 490π

B) $\dfrac{490\pi}{3}$

C) $\dfrac{409\pi}{3}$

D) 160
E) 180

12) DC=6cm. V=120πcm³, what the value of h?

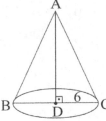

A) 10
B) 11
C) 12
D) 13
E) 16

13) AD=8cm, V=128π. What is the value of DC?

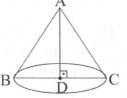

A) $2\sqrt{3}$
B) $3\sqrt{3}$
C) $4\sqrt{3}$
D) $4\sqrt{2}$
E) $4\sqrt{5}$

14) BD=2x, AD=3x. What is the volume of the cone?

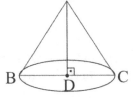

A) $4x^3$
B) $4x^2$
C) $5x^3\pi$
D) $\pi4x^3$
E) $6x^3\pi$

15) DC = $\sqrt{5}$cm, AD = $\sqrt{7}$cm. What is the volume of the cone?

A) $\dfrac{5\pi}{3}$

B) $\dfrac{7\pi}{3}$

C) $\dfrac{5\pi\sqrt{3}}{3}$

D) $\dfrac{7\pi\sqrt{5}}{4}$

E) $\dfrac{5\sqrt{7}\pi}{3}$

TEST 36

(Surface Area and Volume of Spheres)

1) OA=r=11cm. What is the surface area of the sphere?

A) 22π
B) 33π
C) 88π
D) 121
E) 484π

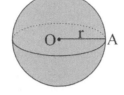

5) AB=12.6cm. What is the surface area of the sphere?

A) 635π
B) 548.76π
C) 160
D) 164π
E) 458

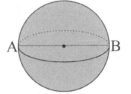

2) OA=13cm. What is the surface area of the sphere?

A) 169π
B) 149π
C) 121π
D) 100π
E) 676π

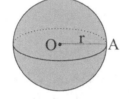

6) The area of sphere $400\pi cm^2$. What is the radius of the sphere?

A) 4
B) 5
C) 6
D) 7
E) 10

3) OA=r=12.2cm. What is the surface area of the sphere?

A) $695.36\,\pi$
B) $595.36\,\pi$
C) 458.85π
D) 368.68π
E) $295.36\,\pi$

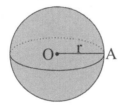

7) The sphere radius is $3\pi cm$. What is the area of a sphere?

A) 36
B) 36π
C) $36\pi^3$
D) 72π
E) $72\pi^3$

4) AB=14cm. What is the surface area of the sphere?

A) 196
B) 196π
C) 49π
D) 49
E) 89π

8) OA=4cm. What is the volume of a sphere? (π=3.14)

A) 200.96
B) 220.96
C) 270.96
D) 290.96
E) 300.96

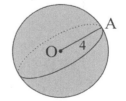

9) OA=3.3cm. What is the volume of a sphere?

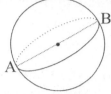

A) 37.7
B) 39
C) 40
D) 41
E) 42

10) AB=20cm. What is the volume of a sphere?

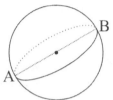

A) 4,167.79
B) 4,187.67
C) 4,188.79
D) 4,444.49
E) 4,560.65

11) The volume of a sphere is $200\pi cm^3$. Find the sphere radius.

A) 5
B) $5\sqrt{6}$
C) $5\sqrt{3}$
D) $4\sqrt{2}$
E) $4\sqrt{3}$

12) Find the sphere volume of the radius is 2πcm.

A) $32\pi^2$
B) $32\pi^3$
C) $32\pi^4$
D) $\dfrac{32\pi^4}{3}$
E) 64π

13) AB=6cm, DC=4cm. What is the ratio of the volume of the first sphere and the volume of the second sphere?

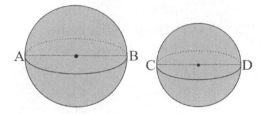

A) $\dfrac{27}{8}$ B) $\dfrac{27}{7}$ C) $\dfrac{28}{7}$

D) $\dfrac{28}{9}$ E) 4

14) OA=r=2.2cm. What is the volume of the sphere?

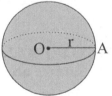

A) 22.3
B) 33.3
C) 44.6
D) 55.6
E) 66.6

15) The sphere volume is $160\pi cm^3$. What is the radius of the sphere?

A) $2\sqrt{15}$
B) $2\sqrt[3]{15}$
C) $3\sqrt{15}$
D) $3\sqrt[3]{15}$
E) $4\sqrt{15}$

TEST 37
(Matrix)

1) $A = \begin{bmatrix} 4 & 3 \\ 2 & 1 \end{bmatrix}, B = \begin{bmatrix} 4 & 5 \\ 3 & 6 \end{bmatrix}, A + B = ?$

A) $\begin{bmatrix} 8 & 8 \\ 5 & 7 \end{bmatrix}$ 　　　 B) $\begin{bmatrix} 8 & 8 \\ 6 & 7 \end{bmatrix}$

C) $\begin{bmatrix} 6 & 7 \\ 8 & 9 \end{bmatrix}$ 　　　 D) $\begin{bmatrix} 7 & 7 \\ 3 & 6 \end{bmatrix}$

E) $\begin{bmatrix} 6 & 8 \\ 10 & 11 \end{bmatrix}$

4) $A = \begin{bmatrix} 6 & 4 \\ 3 & 2 \end{bmatrix}, B = \begin{bmatrix} 2 & 3 \\ 1 & 2 \end{bmatrix}, 3A - 2B = ?$

A) $\begin{bmatrix} 14 & 5 \\ 8 & 4 \end{bmatrix}$ 　　　 B) $\begin{bmatrix} 14 & 6 \\ 7 & 4 \end{bmatrix}$

C) $\begin{bmatrix} 14 & 6 \\ 8 & 2 \end{bmatrix}$ 　　　 D) $\begin{bmatrix} 13 & 6 \\ 8 & 4 \end{bmatrix}$

E) $\begin{bmatrix} 6 & 12 \\ 7 & 3 \end{bmatrix}$

2) $A = \begin{bmatrix} 9 & 11 \\ 7 & 3 \end{bmatrix}, B = \begin{bmatrix} 6 & 4 \\ 3 & 2 \end{bmatrix}, A - B = ?$

A) $\begin{bmatrix} 3 & 4 \\ 4 & 1 \end{bmatrix}$ 　　　 B) $\begin{bmatrix} 3 & 7 \\ 4 & 1 \end{bmatrix}$

C) $\begin{bmatrix} 3 & 7 \\ 1 & 4 \end{bmatrix}$ 　　　 D) $\begin{bmatrix} 6 & 6 \\ 3 & 2 \end{bmatrix}$

E) $\begin{bmatrix} 6 & 4 \\ 3 & 3 \end{bmatrix}$

5) $A = \begin{bmatrix} 6 & 4 \\ 8 & 12 \end{bmatrix}, \quad B = \begin{bmatrix} 8 & 10 \\ 6 & 4 \end{bmatrix},$

$A + B = \begin{bmatrix} 14 & 2x \\ 14 & 4y \end{bmatrix}, \quad x + y = ?$

A) 11　　　 B) 12　　 C) 13
D) 14　　　 E) 15

3) $A = \begin{bmatrix} 4 & 3 \\ 2 & 7 \end{bmatrix}, 3A = ?$

A) $\begin{bmatrix} 4 & 3 \\ 2 & 7 \end{bmatrix}$ 　　　 B) $\begin{bmatrix} 8 & 6 \\ 4 & 14 \end{bmatrix}$

C) $\begin{bmatrix} 12 & 9 \\ 4 & 21 \end{bmatrix}$ 　　　 D) $\begin{bmatrix} 12 & 9 \\ 6 & 21 \end{bmatrix}$

E) $\begin{bmatrix} 12 & 9 \\ 6 & 12 \end{bmatrix}$

6) $A = \begin{bmatrix} 14 & 12 \\ 20 & 16 \end{bmatrix}, \quad B = \begin{bmatrix} 4 & 4 \\ 6 & 6 \end{bmatrix},$

$A - B = \begin{bmatrix} 5x & 8 \\ 7y & 10 \end{bmatrix}, \quad 2x + 3y = ?$

A) 10　　　 B) 11　　 C) 12
D) 13　　　 E) 14

7) $A = \begin{bmatrix} 0 & 1 \\ 3 & 4 \end{bmatrix}, B = \begin{bmatrix} 4 & 3 \\ 2 & 1 \end{bmatrix}, A + B = ?$

A) $\begin{bmatrix} 5 & 4 \\ 6 & 5 \end{bmatrix}$ B) $\begin{bmatrix} 4 & 4 \\ 5 & 5 \end{bmatrix}$

C) $\begin{bmatrix} 3 & 4 \\ 5 & 5 \end{bmatrix}$ D) $\begin{bmatrix} 6 & 4 \\ 2 & 2 \end{bmatrix}$

E) $\begin{bmatrix} 0 & 4 \\ 3 & 7 \end{bmatrix}$

8) $A = \begin{bmatrix} 1 & 2 \\ 3 & 4 \end{bmatrix}, B = \begin{bmatrix} 0 & 2 \\ 1 & 3 \end{bmatrix}.$
What is the AB matrix?

A) $\begin{bmatrix} 3 & 8 \\ 4 & 14 \end{bmatrix}$ B) $\begin{bmatrix} 3 & 8 \\ 14 & 4 \end{bmatrix}$

C) $\begin{bmatrix} 7 & 3 \\ 2 & 1 \end{bmatrix}$ D) $\begin{bmatrix} 3 & 8 \\ 4 & 6 \end{bmatrix}$

E) $\begin{bmatrix} 2 & 6 \\ 4 & 18 \end{bmatrix}$

9) $A = \begin{bmatrix} 1 & 2 & 3 \\ 4 & 6 & 7 \end{bmatrix},$
What is the scalar factor 2?

A) $\begin{bmatrix} 1 & 2 & 6 \\ 8 & 12 & 14 \end{bmatrix}$ B) $\begin{bmatrix} 2 & 4 & 6 \\ 8 & 12 & 14 \end{bmatrix}$

C) $\begin{bmatrix} 2 & 4 & 6 \\ 9 & 12 & 14 \end{bmatrix}$ D) $\begin{bmatrix} 7 & 3 & 2 \\ 4 & 8 & 10 \end{bmatrix}$

E) $\begin{bmatrix} 1 & 4 & 12 \\ 8 & 12 & 14 \end{bmatrix}$

10) $A = \begin{bmatrix} 7 & 5 & 25 \\ 2 & -10 & 9 \end{bmatrix},$
What is the A matrix transpose?

A) $\begin{bmatrix} 7 & 2 \\ 5 & 9 \\ 25 & 10 \end{bmatrix}$ B) $\begin{bmatrix} 7 & 2 \\ 5 & -10 \\ 25 & 9 \end{bmatrix}$

C) $\begin{bmatrix} 7 & 2 \\ 5 & -10 \\ 2 & 9 \end{bmatrix}$ D) $\begin{bmatrix} 7 & 9 \\ 5 & -10 \\ 25 & 2 \end{bmatrix}$

E) $\begin{bmatrix} 6 & 2 \\ 4 & 1 \\ 3 & 7 \end{bmatrix}$

11) What is the transpose of the matrix $\begin{bmatrix} 1 & 2 & 4 \\ 8 & 9 & 10 \end{bmatrix}?$

A) $\begin{bmatrix} 1 & 8 \\ 2 & 9 \\ 4 & 10 \end{bmatrix}$ B) $\begin{bmatrix} 1 & 8 \\ 4 & 9 \\ 2 & 10 \end{bmatrix}$

C) $\begin{bmatrix} 1 & 10 \\ 2 & 9 \\ 4 & 8 \end{bmatrix}$ D) $\begin{bmatrix} 1 & 9 \\ 2 & 9 \\ 4 & 10 \end{bmatrix}$

E) $\begin{bmatrix} 8 & 9 & 10 \\ 1 & 2 & 4 \end{bmatrix}$

12) What is the transpose of the

matrix $\begin{bmatrix} 2 & 4 & 6 \\ 8 & 9 & 10 \\ 11 & 12 & 3 \end{bmatrix}$?

A) $\begin{bmatrix} 2 & 8 & 11 \\ 4 & 9 & 12 \\ 6 & 10 & 13 \end{bmatrix}$ B) $\begin{bmatrix} 2 & 8 & 11 \\ 4 & 9 & 12 \\ 6 & 10 & 3 \end{bmatrix}$

C) $\begin{bmatrix} 2 & 4 & 6 \\ 4 & 9 & 10 \\ 12 & 11 & 3 \end{bmatrix}$ D) $\begin{bmatrix} 2 & 8 & 13 \\ 4 & 9 & 12 \\ 6 & 10 & 11 \end{bmatrix}$

E) $\begin{bmatrix} 2 & 6 & 4 \\ 4 & 10 & 9 \\ 6 & 3 & 12 \end{bmatrix}$

13) $A = \begin{bmatrix} 1 & 2 \\ 3 & 4 \end{bmatrix}$, $B = \begin{bmatrix} 5 & 6 \\ 7 & 8 \end{bmatrix}$,

Then, what is the value of
$A+B^T$?

A) $\begin{bmatrix} 6 & 9 \\ 12 & 9 \end{bmatrix}$ B) $\begin{bmatrix} 6 & 8 \\ 9 & 12 \end{bmatrix}$

C) $\begin{bmatrix} 6 & 9 \\ 9 & 12 \end{bmatrix}$ D) $\begin{bmatrix} 6 & 7 \\ 8 & 9 \end{bmatrix}$

E) $\begin{bmatrix} 3 & 4 \\ 7 & 8 \end{bmatrix}$

14) $A = \begin{bmatrix} 1 & 2 & 3 \\ -2 & 3 & 4 \end{bmatrix}$, $B = \begin{bmatrix} -2 & 4 & 3 \\ 2 & 0 & 1 \end{bmatrix}$,

then, what is the value of
3A+2B?

A) $\begin{bmatrix} -1 & 14 & 15 \\ -2 & 9 & 14 \end{bmatrix}$

B) $\begin{bmatrix} -1 & 14 & 15 \\ 14 & 9 & -2 \end{bmatrix}$

C) $\begin{bmatrix} -1 & 14 & 15 \\ 11 & 12 & 3 \end{bmatrix}$

D) $\begin{bmatrix} 15 & 14 & -1 \\ -2 & 9 & 1 \end{bmatrix}$

E) $\begin{bmatrix} 3 & 4 & 5 \\ 6 & 7 & 8 \end{bmatrix}$

15) $A = \begin{bmatrix} 1 & 2 \\ 3 & 4 \end{bmatrix}$, $B = \begin{bmatrix} 5 & 6 \\ 7 & 8 \end{bmatrix}$,

Then, what is the value of
$2A^T+3B^T$?

A) $\begin{bmatrix} 17 & 27 \\ 0 & 4 \end{bmatrix}$ B) $\begin{bmatrix} 17 & 27 \\ 22 & 23 \end{bmatrix}$

C) $\begin{bmatrix} 17 & 27 \\ 22 & 32 \end{bmatrix}$ D) $\begin{bmatrix} 17 & 17 \\ 0 & 4 \end{bmatrix}$

E) $\begin{bmatrix} 16 & 17 & 27 \\ 4 & 3 & 2 \end{bmatrix}$

TEST 38
(Mixed Geometry Problems)

Use the following information for questions 1-4.

The rectangular prism with height 4cm, length 10cm and width are 12cm.

1) What is the volume of the rectangular prism?

A) $480cm^3$ B) $420cm^3$
C) $380cm^3$ D) $320cm^3$
E) $280cm^3$

2) What is the surface area of the rectangular prism?

A) $406cm^2$ B) $416cm^2$
C) $426cm^2$ D) $436cm^2$
E) $446cm^2$

3) What is the lateral surface area of the rectangular prism?

A) $146cm^2$ B) $156cm^2$
C) $166cm^2$ D) $176cm^2$
E) $186cm^2$

4) What is the sum of the top area of the rectangular prism and bottom area of the rectangular prism?

A) $240cm^2$ B) $220cm^2$
C) $210cm^2$ D) $200cm^2$
E) $190cm^2$

Use the following information for questions 5-7.

The cylinder diameter is 10cm and height 8cm.

5) What is the sum of the top area of the cylinder and bottom area of the cylinder?

A) 25π B) 30π C) 40π
D) 50π E) 60π

6) What is the volume of the cylinder?

A) 100π B) 200π C) 220π
D) 240π E) 260π

7) What is the surface area of the cylinder?

A) 329.87   B) 408.40
C) 430.20   D) 436.10
E) 436.20

Use the following information for questions 8-9.

The radius of the cylinder is 4cm, and height is 6cm.

8) What is the base area of the cylinder?

A) 4π B) 8π C) 16π
D) 20π E) 24π

9) What is the volume of the cylinder?

A) 96π B) 86π C) 76π

D) 66π E) 56π

Use the following information for questions 10-12.

The base area of the cylinder is $64\pi \text{cm}^2$ and the height is 5cm.

10) What is the diameter of the cylinder?

A) 12   B) 16   C) 18

D) 32   E) 40

11) What is the volume of the cylinder?

A) 300π B) 310π C) 320π

D) 340π E) 350π

12) What is the lateral surface area of the cylinder?

A) 80π B) 70π C) 60π

D) 50π E) 40π

13) The altitude of an equilateral triangle is $12\sqrt{3}$ cm. What is the length of a side?

A) 18   B) 20   C) 22

D) 24   E) 32

Use the following information for questions 14-15.

ABC is an isosceles right triangle which is a 45^0-45^0-90^0 triangle. The length of the hypotenuse is 6cm.

14) What is the side length of the triangle?

A) 3   B) $3\sqrt{3}$ C) $3\sqrt{2}$

D) $3\sqrt{5}$ E) 4

15) What is the area of the triangle?

A) 5   B) 6

C) 7   D) 8

E) 9

TEST 39
(Mixed Geometry Problems)

Use the following figure for questions 1-5.

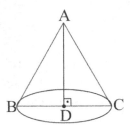

BC=16cm and AC=10cm.

1) **What is the height of the cone?**

   A) 5cm   B) 6cm   C) 7cm
   D) 8cm   E) 9cm

2) **What is the base area of the cone?**

   A) 16π B) 32π C) 64π
   D) 128π E) 256π

3) **What is the volume of the cone?**

   A) 128π B) 130π C) 140π
   D) 168π E) 180π

4) **What is the surface area of the cone?**

   A) 120π B) 132π C) 140π
   D) 144π E) 160π

5) **What is the slant height of the cone?**

   A) 10   B) 12   C) 13
   D) 26   E) 30

Use the following figure for questions 6-9.

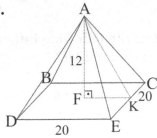

DE=EC=20cm, AF=height=12cm. AK=slant height.

6) **What is the volume of the pyramid?**

   A) 1,600   B) 1,500   C) 1,400
   D) 1,300   E) 1,200

7) **What is the base area of the pyramid?**

   A) 300.56   B) 400.56   C) 619.56
   D) 624.82   E) 699.56

8) **What is the lateral surface area of the pyramid?**

   A) 624.82cm^2 B) 625.45cm^2
   C) 630cm^2 D) 1,040cm^2
   E) 950.82cm^2

9) **What is the surface area of the pyramid?**

   A) 600.56cm^2 B) 610cm^2
   C) 630cm^2 D) 1,040cm^2
   E) 1,024.82cm^2

Use the following figure for the question and 10 and question 11.

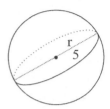

The figure is a sphere. r=5cm.

10) What is the surface area of the sphere?

A) 25π B) 50π C) 75π

D) 100π E) 125π

11) What is the volume of the sphere?

A) 500π B) $\dfrac{500\pi}{7}$ C) $\dfrac{500\pi}{3}$

D) 250π E) 400π

12) What is the ratio of the vole of the sphere and the volume of the cube? (a=r)

A) $\dfrac{4}{3}$ B) $\dfrac{4}{3}\pi$ C) $\dfrac{3}{4}\pi$

D) $\dfrac{16}{9}\pi$ E) $\dfrac{9}{16}\pi$

13) $x^2-8x+y^2-10y=1$. What is the center point of the circle?

A) (4, 5) B) (–5, –4)
C) (–5, 4) D) (3, –4)
E) (–3, –4)

14) What is the equation of the circle with the center of (3, –2) and radius 7?

A) $x^2+y^2-6x+8y-36=0$
B) $x^2+y^2-6x+4y-36=0$
C) $x^2+y^2-6x-4y+33=0$
D) $x^2+y^2-8x+6y+36=0$
E) $x^2+y^2-8x-6y+36=0$

15) The circle in the XY-plane has a diameter with endpoints at (6, 12) and (–4, –2). Which of the following is the center of the circle?

A) (–1, 5) B) (5, –1)
C) (1, 5) D) (–2, 6)
E) (–2, –6)

TEST 40
(Mixed Geometry Problems)

1) $\angle A$ and $\angle B$ are complementary angles. If $m\angle A=6x-4$ and $m\angle B=4x+6$. What is the value of $m\angle B$?

A) 41.2^0 B) 42.6^0 C) 42.8^0
D) 44.4^0 E) 45^0

2) $\angle A$ and $\angle B$ are complementary angles. If $m\angle A=3x+4$ and $m\angle B=x+6$. What is the value of $m\angle A$?

A) 45^0 B) 60^0 C) 64^0
D) 70^0 E) 90^0

3) $\angle C$ and $\angle D$ are complementary angles. If $m\angle C=6x+4$ and $m\angle D=3x-6$. What is the value of $\angle D$?

A) 16^0 B) 20^0 C) 22.47^0
D) 24.67^0 E) 25.67^0

4) $\angle K$ and $\angle L$ are complementary angles. If $\angle K:\angle L=1/4$. What is the value of $\angle K$?

A) 12^0 B) 16^0 C) 18^0
D) 20^0 E) 24^0

5) $\angle J$ and $\angle K$ are complementary angles. If $\angle J:\angle K=1/5$. What is the value of $\angle K$?

A) 75^0 B) 80^0 C) 85^0
D) 90^0 E) 120^0

6) $\angle P$ and $\angle K$ are supplementary angles. If $\angle P=2x$ and $m\angle K=3x$. What is the value of $\angle P$?

A) 72^0 B) 76^0 C) 80^0
D) 84^0 E) 96^0

7) $\angle A$ and $\angle B$ are supplementary angles. $\angle A-\angle B=20^0$. What is the value of $\angle B$?

A) 40^0 B) 56^0 C) 60^0
D) 80^0 E) 90^0

8) $\angle K$ and $\angle M$ are supplementary angles. If $\angle K:\angle M=1/4$. What is the value of $\angle M$?

A) 64^0 B) 128^0 C) 136^0
D) 144^0 E) 156^0

9) $\angle J$ and $\angle K$ are supplementary angles. If $\angle J - \angle K=30^0$. What is the value of $\angle K$?

A) 60^0 B) 70^0 C) 75^0
D) 84^0 E) 96^0

10) C is the midpoint of $\overrightarrow{AB}$. $AC=6x+14$ and $BC=4x+36$. What is the value of AB?

A) 120   B) 160   C) 180
D) 200   E) 220

Use the following figure for question 11 and question 12.

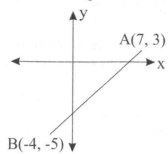

11) What is the distance AB?

   A) $\sqrt{185}$ B) $\sqrt{195}$ C) $\sqrt{215}$

   D) 15   E) $\sqrt{235}$

12) What is the midpoint of the AB?

   A) $\left(\dfrac{2}{3}, -1\right)$ B) $\left(\dfrac{3}{2}, -1\right)$

   C) (-1, 2)   D) (2, -1)

   E) $\left(\dfrac{2}{5}, -2\right)$

13) What is the standard equation of the circle with center (5, -3) and radius 7cm?

   A) $(x–3)^2+(y–5)^2=49$

   B) $(x–5)^2+(y+3)^2=49$

   C) $(x–5)^2+(y–3)^2=7$

   D) $(x–3)^2+(y–3)^2=49$

   E) $(x–5)^2+(y–5)^2=49$

14) What is the radius of the circle for $(x–5)^2+(y–12)^2=169$?

   A) 10   B) 11   C) 12

   D) 13   E) 15

15) The perimeter of the square is 8n. What is the area of the square?

   A) $4n^3$ B) $4n^2$ C) 4n

   D) 4   E) 16

TEST 41
(Mixed Geometry Problems)

1) **What is the perimeter in feet of the rectangle with width 10 and length 25?**

A) 35   B) 40   C) 50
D) 70   E) 90

2) **What is the perimeter of the right triangle with the side of 9 cm and 12 cm?**

A) 36   B) 35   C) 32
D) 30   E) 21

Use the following figure for question 3 and question 4.

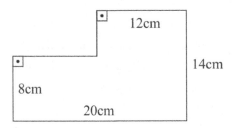

3) **What is the perimeter of the figure?**

A) 60cm   B) 68cm   C) 70cm
D) 72cm   E) 76cm

4) **What is the area of the figure?**

A) 212cm^2 B) 222cm^2
C) 232cm^2 D) 242cm^2
E) 252cm^2

Use the following information for question 5 and question 6.

Two similar triangles have perimeters in the ratio is 7 to 4. The small triangle perimeter is 16cm.

5) **What is the perimeter of the bigger triangle?**

A) 16   B) 21   C) 24
D) 28   E) 32

6) **What is the ratio of the area of the bigger triangle and the area of the small triangle?**

A) $\dfrac{7}{16}$ B) $\dfrac{49}{16}$ C) $\dfrac{49}{10}$

D) $\dfrac{28}{16}$ E) 2

7) **ABCD is a rhombus. AC and BD are diagonal. AC=12 and BD=16cm. What is the perimeter of the rhombus?**

A) 30   B) 40   C) 42
D) 52   E) 56

8) **$(x+3)^2+(y-4)^2=5$. What is the center point of the circle?**

A) (3, 4)   B) (-3, 4)   C) (4, 3)
D) (-4, 3)   E) (-3, -4)

9) A triangle has one side of 14cm and another side of 18cm. What is the possible length of the third side of the triangle?

A) 4 B) 28 C) 32
D) 34 E) 36

10) In similar polygons. The ratio of the area of the polygons is $\frac{4}{9}$. What is the ratio of the volume of the polygons?

A) $\frac{8}{27}$ B) $\frac{2}{3}$ C) $\frac{4}{9}$

D) $\frac{9}{16}$ E) $\frac{4}{5}$

11) What is the center of the circle with a diameter whose endpoint is (6, 8) and (10, 12)?

A) (8, 10) B) (10, 8)
C) (6, 12) D) (10, 18)
E) (10, 6)

Use the following information for question 12 and question 13.

ABCD is a rectangle. AB=x and BC=x+6.

12) What is the perimeter of the rectangle ABCD?

A) 4x B) 6x C) 4x+6
D) 4x+12 E) 4x+8

13) What is the area of the rectangle ABCD?

A) x^2+4 B) x^2+12 C) x^2+12x
D) x^2+6x E) x^2+2

Use the following information for question 14 and question 15.

ABCD is rectangle. DC=2x+4, DC=12cm, and BC=4cm.

14) What is the value of x?

A) 3 B) 4 C) 5
D) 6 E) 7

15) What is the perimeter of the rectangle ABCD?

A) 32 B) 34 C) 36
D) 38 E) 40

TEST 42
(Mixed Geometry Problems)

1) What is the distance between the points A(6, 4) and B(8, 3)?

A) $\sqrt{5}$ B) 5   C) $\sqrt{6}$
D) 6   E) 3

2) What is the distance between the points A(9, 1) and B(6, 4)?

A) 3   B) $3\sqrt{2}$ C) 4
D) $4\sqrt{2}$ E) 6

3) What is the distance between the points K(12, 3) and L(4, 5)?

A) $2\sqrt{14}$ B) $2\sqrt{13}$ C) $2\sqrt{17}$
D) $2\sqrt{19}$ E) $2\sqrt{18}$

4) What is the distance between the points M(9, 1) and K(-3, -4)?

A) 10   B) 11   C) 12
D) 13   E) 14

5) What is the distance between the points A(-6, -3) and B(4, 2)?

A) 4   B) $4\sqrt{5}$ C) 5
D) $5\sqrt{5}$ E) 6

6) What is the distance between the points A(-7, 3) and B(9, 2)?

A) $\sqrt{257}$ B) $\sqrt{167}$ C) $\sqrt{267}$
D) $\sqrt{287}$ E) $\sqrt{187}$

Use the following graph for questions 7-9.

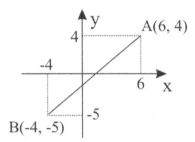

7) What is the distance between the point A and point B?

A) $\sqrt{161}$ B) $\sqrt{171}$ C) $\sqrt{181}$
D) $\sqrt{191}$ E) $\sqrt{201}$

8) What is the slope between the points?

A) $\dfrac{10}{9}$ B) $\dfrac{9}{10}$ C) $-\dfrac{10}{9}$
D) $-\dfrac{9}{10}$ E) 1

9) What is the midpoint between point A and point B?

A) (-2, -3)   B) $\left(-\dfrac{1}{2}, 1\right)$

C) (2, 3)   D) $\left(1, -\dfrac{1}{2}\right)$

E) (1, 2)

Use the following graph for questions 10-12.

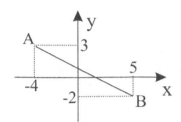

10) What is the distance between the points A and B?

A) $\sqrt{101}$ B) $\sqrt{102}$ C) $\sqrt{103}$
D) $\sqrt{106}$ E) $\sqrt{107}$

11) What is the slope of the line segment between the point A and the point B?

A) $-\dfrac{5}{9}$ B) $\dfrac{5}{9}$ C) $\dfrac{9}{5}$

D) $-\dfrac{9}{5}$ E) $\dfrac{8}{5}$

12) What is the midpoint between the point A and the point B?

A) $\left(2, \dfrac{1}{2}\right)$ B) $\left(2, -\dfrac{1}{2}\right)$

C) $\left(\dfrac{1}{2}, \dfrac{1}{2}\right)$ D) $\left(\dfrac{1}{3}, 2\right)$

E) (1, 1)

13) What is the slope of any line parallel to the line 3x+6y=18?

A) –3   B) –6   C) –2
D) $-\dfrac{1}{2}$ E) –4

14) What is the length of the cube box with surface area 150cm^2?

A) 3   B) 4   C) 5
D) 6   E) 7

15) What is the volume of the cylinder of the height 10cm and diameter of 5cm?

A) 62   B) 62.5   C) 62.5π
D) 6.25π   E) 65π

TEST 43
(Mixed Geometry Problems)

1) **What is the slope of the equation for 3x+6y-65=0?**

   A) 3   B) –3   C) 6

   D) $-\dfrac{1}{2}$ E) 8

2) **ax+4y+16=0 and Slope=$\dfrac{1}{2}$.**

   What is the value of an in the equation?

   A) –2   B) 2   C) 3

   D) $\dfrac{1}{3}$ E) –3

3) **What is the slope between the point A(-3, -4) and point B(8, 9)?**

   A) $\dfrac{13}{11}$ B) $\dfrac{11}{13}$ C) $\dfrac{14}{13}$

   D) $\dfrac{13}{14}$ E) $\dfrac{12}{13}$

4) **What is the slope of the equation for 4x-2y+8=0?**

   A) 4   B) -2   C) $\dfrac{1}{4}$

   D) $-\dfrac{1}{2}$ E) 2

5) **What is the y-intercept of the equation for 5x+10y+20=0?**

   A) 1   B) 2   C) 0

   E) -1   E) -2

6) **What is the equation of the line passing through the point (2, 3) with a slope of 5?**

   A) y=5x–7   B) y=2x–7
   C) y= –5x+7   D) y=7x–2
   E) y=7x+2

7) **What is the equation of the line passing through the point (-2, -4) with a slope of 3?**

   A) y= –3x+2   B) y=3x+2
   C) y=2x+5   D) y=–2x+3
   E) y=2x+3

8) **What is the slope of the equation for 3x+9y+18=0?**

   A) –3   B) $-\dfrac{1}{3}$ C) 9

   D) $-\dfrac{1}{9}$ E) –9

9) **What is the equation of the line that passes through (2, 4) and (1, 3)?**

   A) y=3x+2   B) y=x+5
   C) y=x–2   D) y=x+2
   E) y=2x+5

10) **What is the equation of the line that passes through (6, 3) and (2, 5)?**

   A) y=x–3   B) y=x+3
   C) y=2x–3   D) y=x–7
   E) y=2x+3

Use the following graph for question 11 and question 12.

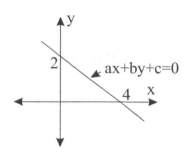

11) What is the value of a+b–c?

A) 1   B) 3.5   C) –1.5
D) –2   E) 2.5

12) What is the equation of the line?

A) x+y=4   B) x+2y=–4
C) x+y=–8   D) x+2y–4=0
E) x+2y+4=0

13) What is the midpoint of (4, 8) and (6, - 4)?

A) (5, -4)   B) (5, 2)   C) (5, -2)
D) (6, 3)   E) (6, -2)

14) ∠A and ∠B are supplementary angles. ∠A:∠B=1:5. What is the value of ∠A?

A) 25^0 B) 28^0 C) 30^0
D) 32^0 E) 36^0

15) Which is the wrong statement?

A) The angle which measures less than 90^0 is called an acute angle

B) The angle which measures 90^0 is called right angle

C) The angle which measures 180^0 is called a straight angle

D) If the sum of two angles measure $180^{0,}$ then it is called supplementary angle

E) If the sum of two angles measures $360^{0,}$ then it is called complementary angle.

TEST 44
(Mixed Geometry Problems)

1) **Which angle is less than 90^0?**

A) Acute angle
B) Right angle
C) Straight angle
D) Supplementary angle
E) Complementary angle

2) **Which angle is between 90^0 and 180^0?**

A) Right angle
B) Acute angle
C) Obtuse angle
D) Full angle
E) Wide angle

3) **Which angle is equal to 180^0?**

A) Right angle
B) Acute angle
C) Straight angle
D) Full angle
E) Obtuse angle

4) **Complete the statement.**
An equilateral triangle has three ___ sides.

A) Equal
B) Isosceles
C) Different
D) Scalene
E) No equal

5) **Complete the statement.**
A scalene triangle has _____ sides.
A) No equal
B) Equilateral
C) Isosceles
D) Perpendicular
E) Equal

6) **Which is a not type of angles?**

A) Acute   B) Right
C) Obtuse   D) Straight
E) Perpendicular

7) **Complete the statement.**

_____ lines are lines that intersect at right angles.

A) Right   B) Perpendicular
C) Parallel   D) Horizontal
E) Vertical

8) **What type of the triangle has the following characteristic?**
All sides are different, and all angles are different.

A) Isosceles
B) Scalene
C) Equilateral
D) Right angle
E) Perpendicular

9) **What type of the triangle has the following characteristic?**
The two sides and two angles are congruent.

A) Right triangle
B) Scalene triangle
C) Isosceles triangle
D) Equilateral triangle
E) Acute triangle

10) What type of the geometric figure has the following characteristic?
Opposite sides are parallel and all sides are equal.

A) Rectangular
B) Triangle
C) Trapezoid
D) Square
E) Right triangle

11) What is the ratio of the straight angle and full angle?

A) 1   B) $\dfrac{1}{2}$ C) 3

D) $\dfrac{1}{3}$ E) 2

12) Complete the statement.
The area of the triangle is _____ times the product of base and height?

A) 0.5   B) 2   C) 2
D) 4   E) 6

13) What is the volume of the cube with surface area 300cm^2?

A) $250\sqrt{2}$ B) $230\sqrt{2}$
C) $200\sqrt{2}$ D) 250
E) 480

14) The rectangular prism has sides of length 2cm, 6cm, and 8cm. What is the volume of the rectangular prism?

A) 72cm^3 B) 84cm^3 C) 90cm^3
D) 96cm^3 E) 100cm^3

15) The rectangular prism has sides of length 4.5cm, 5cm, and 10cm. What is the volume of the rectangular prism?

A) 180cm^3 B) 200cm^3
C) 225cm^3 D) 250cm^3
E) 260cm^3

TEST 45
(Mixed Geometry Problems)

1) The circle has a diameter of 10cm. What is the area of the circle?

A) 100π B) 50π C) 25π
D) 10π E) 5π

2) The circle has a radius of 6cm. What is the area of the circle?

A) 6π B) 12π C) 24π
D) 36π E) 42π

3) The circumference is 12πcm. What is the area of the circle?

A) 36 B) 36π C) 42π
D) 48π E) 48π

4) What is the circumference of the circle with the area of 64πcm^2?

A) 12π B) 14π C) 15π
D) 16π E) 20π

5) What is the area of a circle radius of $\dfrac{6}{\pi}$cm?

A) $\dfrac{6}{\pi}$ B) $\dfrac{12}{\pi}$ C) $\dfrac{36}{\pi}$
D) 36π E) 40π

6) What is the surface area of a cube with each side of a?

A) $6a^2$ B) $8a^2$ C) $9a^2$
D) $6a$ E) $9a$

7) The surface area of a cube is 150cm^2. What is the volume of the cube?

A) 100 B) 125 C) 150
D) 180 E) 225

Use the following information for questions 8-10.

The length of the edge of the cube is 7cm.

8) What is the volume of the cube?

A) 323cm^3 B) 333cm^3
C) 343cm^3 D) 364cm^3
E) 372cm^3

9) What is the surface area of the cube?

A) 274cm^2 B) 276cm^2
C) 294cm^2 D) 284cm^2
E) 286cm^2

10) What is the lateral surface area of the cube?

A) 198cm^2 B) 186cm^2
C) 176cm^2 D) 166cm^2
E) 156cm^2

Use the following information for questions 11-12.

The length of the edge of a cube is 0.3cm.

11) What is the surface area of the cube?

A) 54cm^2 B) 5.4cm^2
C) 0.54cm^2 D) 540cm^2
E) 544cm^2

12) What is the volume of the cube?

A) 27cm^3 B) 2.7cm^3
C) 0.27cm^3 D) 0.027cm^3
E) 270cm^3

13) What is the surface area of a cube with edge length 10cm?

A) 600   B) 620   C) 640
D) 660   E) 680

14) What is the surface area of a cube with edge length 12cm?

A) 724   B) 824   C) 864
D) 942   E) 954

15) What is the volume of a cube with surface area 96cm^2?

A) 56   B) 60   C) 64
D) 72   E) 76

TEST 46
(Mixed Geometry Problems)

1) **The pairs of rectangles are similar. What is the value of x?**

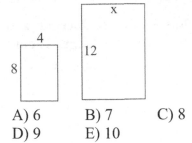

A) 6   B) 7   C) 8
D) 9   E) 10

2) **The pairs of rectangles are similar. What is the value of x?**

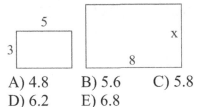

A) 4.8   B) 5.6   C) 5.8
D) 6.2   E) 6.8

3) **The pairs of triangles are similar. What is the value of x?**

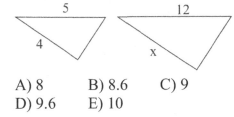

A) 8   B) 8.6   C) 9
D) 9.6   E) 10

4) **The pairs of triangles are similar. What is the value of x?**

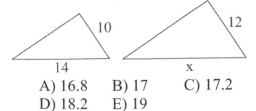

A) 16.8   B) 17   C) 17.2
D) 18.2   E) 19

5) **What is the value of x?**

A) 12
B) 13
C) 16.8
D) 18
E) 19

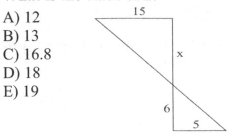

6) **What is the value of x?**

A) 12
B) 12.4
C) 13
D) 14.4
E) 14.6

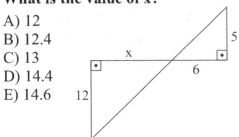

Use the following figure for question 7 and question 8.

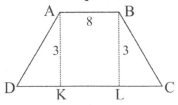

7) **If DK and LC=4 cm, what is the value of AD+BC?**

A) 10   B) 11   C) 12
D) 13   E) 15

8) **What is the perimeter of the trapezoid ABCD?**

A) 24   B) 28   C) 30
D) 34   E) 36

9) What is the area of the trapezoid ABCD?

A) 30   B) 32   C) 36
D) 38   E) 40

Use the following information and figure for question 10-11.

AD is perpendicular to BC.

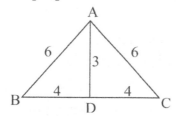

10) What is the perimeter of all triangles?

A) 40   B) 42   C) 46
D) 48   E) 52

11) What is the area of triangle ABC?

A) 9   B) 9.6   C) 10
D) 12   E) 13

12) What is the surface area of the cube?

A) 384cm^2
B) 394cm^2
C) 396cm^2
D) 424cm^2
E) 496cm^2

8cm

8cm

8cm

13) What is the circumference of the base of a cone with height 20cm and slant height 25cm?

A) 20π   B) 24π   C) 30π
D) 32π   E) 40π

14) What is the radius of the base of the cone with height 8cm and slant height 10cm?

A) 6   B) 7   C) 8
D) 9   E) 10

15) What is the height of triangular prism whose base area is 24cm^2 and whose volume 120cm^3?

A) 5   B) 8   C) 10
D) 16   E) 18

TEST 47
(Mixed Geometry Problems)

1) **What is the midpoint between the points A(-6, 4) and B(-2, 8)?**

   A) (-4, 5)   B) (-4, 6)   C) (4, -6)
   D) (-3, 7)   E) (4, -7)

2) **What is the coordinates of the midpoint of point A(-8, 4) and point B(4, 2)?**

   A) (2, 3)   B) (-2, 3)   C) (2, 4)
   D) (1, 2)   E) (1, -2)

3) **What is the coordinates of the midpoint of point A(6, 9) and point B(2, 3)?**

   A) (6, 4)   B) (4, 5)   C) (4, 6)
   D) (-4, 2)   E) (4, -2)

4) **Line segment KM has midpoint L. The coordinates of point K are (-4, 8), and the coordinates of point L are (-2, 6). What are the coordinates of point M?**

   A) (0, 4)   B) (0, 6)   C) (4, 0)
   D) (-4, 2)   E) (4, -2)

5) **What is the distance between point A(-4, 8) and point B(2, 3)?**

   A) 61   B) $\sqrt{61}$ C) $\sqrt{31}$
   D) 31   E) 41

6) **What is the distance between the point A(7, 3) and point B(-1, -3)?**

   A) 10   B) 100   C) $\sqrt{90}$
   D) $\sqrt{74}$ E) 9

7) **What is the distance between point A(15, 16) and point B(3, 6)?**

   A) $\sqrt{240}$ B) $\sqrt{244}$ C) $\sqrt{304}$
   D) $\sqrt{344}$ E) $\sqrt{354}$

8) **Which of the following is a wrong statement?**

   A) 5 sides – Pentagon
   B) 6 sides – Hexagon
   C) 7 sides - Heptagon
   D) 9 sides – Octagon
   E) 8 sides – Octagon

Use the following table to answer the question 9 and question 10.

Polygon	Sides	A	B	Sum of exterior angles
Any polygon	n	(n-2)·180	(n-2)·180) /n	360^0

9) **What is the representing of A in the table?**

   A) Sum of interior angles
   B) Sides
   C) Sum of exterior angles
   D) Each interior angle of a regular polygon
   E) Perimeter of polygon

10) What is the representing of B in the table?

A) Sum of interior angles
B) Each interior angle of a regular polygon
C) Sum of exterior angles
D) Sum of Perimeter
E) Area of a regular polygon

Use the following information and figure for question 11 and question 12.

The figure is a regular hexagon.

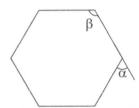

11) What is the value of α?

A) 60   B) 70   C) 80
D) 110   E) 120

12) What is the value of β?

A) 80   B) 90   C) 100
D) 120   E) 140

13) What is the base area of the square pyramid with base edge lengths 5cm?

A) $10cm^2$ B) $15cm^2$ C) $25cm^2$
D) $50cm^2$ E) $75cm^2$

14) What is the slant height of the cone with base radius 12cm and height 16cm?

A) 16cm   B) 18cm   C) 22cm
D) 20cm   E) 24cm

15) What is the circumference of a cone with base area $9\pi cm^2$?

A) 4π B) 6π C) 8π
D) 12π E) 18π

TEST 48

(Mixed Geometry Problems)

1) What is the value of x?

A) 4
B) 5
C) 6
D) 7
E) 8

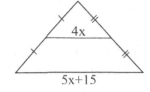

2) What is the value of x?

A) 7
B) 8
C) 9
D) 10
E) 11

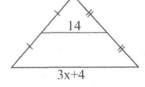

Use the following figure for question 3 and question 4.

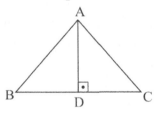

3) BD=DC. AB=6x, and AC=4x+8. What is the value of x?

A) 1   B) 2   C) 3
D) 4   E) 5

4) What is the value of AC?

A) 24   B) 36   C) 48
D) 52   E) 56

5) The exterior angle of a regular polygon is 30⁰. What is the number of sides of the polygon?

A) 8   B) 10   C) 11
D) 12   E) 14

6) The interior angle of a regular polygon is 150⁰. What is the number of sides of the polygon?

A) 12   B) 16   C) 18
D) 20   E) 22

7) What is the value of CD?

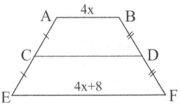

A) 4x+4   B) 4x+8   C) 8x+4
D) 2x+4   E) x+4

8) What is the measure of each interior angle of the regular 15-gon?

A) 145   B) 156   C) 165
D) 166   E) 169

9) What is the sum of the interior angles of a 12-gon?

A) 1,200⁰   B) 1,600⁰   C) 1,800⁰
D) 2,200⁰   E) 2,400⁰

10) The exterior angle of a regular polygon is 18^0. What is the number of sides of the polygon?

A) 20   B) 24   C) 36

D) 40   E) 42

Use the following figure for question 11 and question 12.

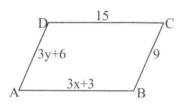

11) What is the value of x?

A) 3   B) 3.2   C) 4

D) 4.4   E) 5

12) What is the value of y?

A) 3   B) 2   C) 2.4

D) 1   E) 0.6

13) What is the center point of the circle for $x^2+y^2+4x+8y-8=0$?

A) (–2, 4)   B) (–2, –4)

C) (–4, 2)   D) (–4, 6)

E) (–4, –6)

14) What is the radius of the circle for $x^2+y^2+4x+8y-56=0$?

A) 6   B) $3\sqrt{13}$ C) $4\sqrt{13}$

D) $5\sqrt{13}$ E) 8

15) What is the center point of the circle for $x^2-6x+y^2-18y=4$?

A) (–3, 8)   B) (9, –3)

C) (8, –3)   D) (3, 9)

E) (–8, –3)

TEST 49

(Mixed Geometry Problems)

Use the following information and figure for questions 1-4.

ABCD is parallelogram. AK=4cm, BC=4x+2, AD=8cm, AB=15cm, DC=4y-5.

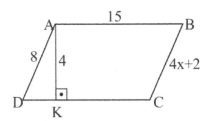

1) What is the value of x?

A) 3.5   B) 2.5   C) 2.6
D) 2   E) 1.5

2) What is the value of y?

A) 2   B) 3   C) 4
D) 5   E) 6

3) What is the area of the parallelogram ABCD?

A) 56   B) 58   C) 60
D) 64   E) 68

4) What is the value of DK?

A) $2\sqrt{3}$ B) $3\sqrt{3}$ C) $4\sqrt{3}$
D) $5\sqrt{3}$ E) $6\sqrt{3}$

Use the following information and figure for questions 5-7.

ABCD is a rhombus. DK=3cm, KC=4cm.

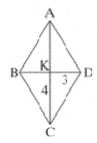

5) What is the value of AC+BD?

A) 12   B) 13   C) 14
D) 15   E) 16

6) What is the value of AB+BC?

A) 9   B) 10   C) 11
D) 12   E) 13

7) What is the area of rhombus ABCD?

A) 24   B) 26   C) 28
D) 30   E) 32

8) Complete the following statement.
The area of_____ is half of the product of diagonals.

A) Square   B) Rectangle
C) Rhombus   D) Triangle
E) Trapezoid

9) Complete the following statement.

The volume of_____ is the product of the length, the width, and the height.

A) Triangular prism
B) Cube
C) Rectangular prism
D) Cylinder
E) Pyramid

Use the following information and figure for questions 10-12.

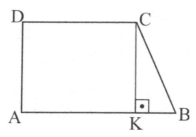

DC=10cm, BC=5cm, and AB=13cm.

10) What is the value of AD?

A) 2   B) 3   C) 4
D) 6   E) 8

11) What is the perimeter of the trapezoid ABCD?

A) 28cm   B) 30cm   C) 31cm
D) 32cm   E) 36cm

12) What is the area of the trapezoid ABCD?

A) 30   B) 32   C) 34
D) 36   E) 46

13) The length of a rectangle is 4cm, and the length of diagonal of the rectangle is 8cm. What is the area of the rectangle?

A) $16\sqrt{3}$ B) $4\sqrt{3}$ C) $2\sqrt{3}$
D) 14   E) 16.2

Use the following information for questions 14-15.

The perimeter of a rectangular is 42cm. The ratio of lengths of two sides is 3:4.

14) What is the area of the rectangle?

A) 108   B) 104   C) 100
D) 96   E) 84

15) What is the perimeter of the rectangle?

A) 8   B) 15   C) 16
D) 30   E) 42

TEST 50
(Mixed Geometry Problems)

1) Two sides of the triangle have lengths 9 and 12cm. What is the largest possible integer value for the length of the third side?

A) 18   B) 20   C) 23
D) 24   E) 25

2) What is the area of the square with a diagonal of length 20cm?

A) 200   B) 250   C) 300
D) 400   E) 500

3) In $\triangle ABC$, AB=AC=20cm and BC=24cm. What is the area of the triangle ABC?

A) 156   B) 186   C) 192
D) 194   E) 208

Use the following information for question 4-5.

In a 30^0-60^0-90^0 triangle, the side opposite to the 30^0 angles has length 8cm.

4) What is the area of the triangle?

A) $24\sqrt{3}$ B) $30\sqrt{3}$ C) $26\sqrt{3}$
D) $32\sqrt{3}$ E) $16\sqrt{3}$

5) What is the perimeter of the triangle?

A) $24+8\sqrt{3}$ B) $12+8\sqrt{3}$
C) $18\sqrt{3}$ D) $17+8\sqrt{3}$
E) $28\sqrt{3}$

6) The ratio of the sides of the triangle is 2:4:6. What is the length of the smallest side if the perimeter is 48cm?

A) 8   B) 10   C) 11
D) 12   E) 13

7) What is the area of the square with a diagonal of length $6\sqrt{2}$ cm?

A) 22   B) 24   C) 36
D) 38   E) 40

8) What is the perimeter of the square with the area is $36x^2$ cm^2?

A) 12x   B) 16x   C) 20x
D) 24x   E) 26x

9) The area of a rectangle with sides of length x and x+1 is 20cm^2. What is the perimeter of the rectangular?

A) 12   B) 14   C) 16
D) 18   E) 20

10) The area of rectangular is 30cm^2, and its perimeter is 22cm. What is the length of a diagonal of the rectangle?

A) $\sqrt{41}$ B) $2\sqrt{21}$ C) $\sqrt{61}$
D) $6\sqrt{21}$ E) $\sqrt{71}$

11) What is the area of the right triangle with base 16cm and height 12cm?

A) 52cm^2 B) 62cm^2
C) 72cm^2 D) 96cm^2
E) 160cm^2

12) What is the area of a rhombus with diagonals of length 20cm and 32cm?

A) 240cm^2 B) 300cm^2
C) 320cm^2 D) 360cm^2
E) 420cm^2

13) A parallelogram with an area of 84cm^2 has a base that measures 7cm. What is the height of the parallelogram?

A) 9cm   B) 10cm   C) 11cm
D) 12cm   E) 13cm

14) The area of the triangle is 96cm^2; the height is 12cm. What is the length of the base of the triangle?

A) 16cm   B) 12cm   C) 8cm
D) 10cm   E) 14cm

15) The area of the rectangle is 288cm^2 and lengths are 24cm. What is the other side?

A) 10cm   B) 11cm   C) 12cm
D) 13cm   E) 14cm

TEST 51
(Mixed Geometry Problems)

1) **Complete the following statement.**

The area of_____ is half of the product of the base and height.

A) Square   B) Rectangle
C) Rhombus   D) Triangle
E) Trapezoid

2) **Which is not a correct statement?**

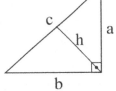

A) The area is $(a+b)\times\dfrac{1}{2}$

B) The perimeter is a+b+c

C) The Pythagorean Theorem is $a^2+b^2=c^2$

D) The area is 0.5(axb)

E) The area is half of the product of a and b.

Use the following information and figure for questions 3-5.

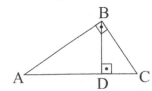

AB=6cm, BC=8cm.

3) **What is the value of AC?**

A) 9   B) 10   C) 11
D) 12   E) 14

4) **What is the area of triangle ABC?**

A) 48   B) 38   C) 24
D) 22   E) 20

5) **If the CD is 4cm, what is the value of BD?**

A) 6.83   B) 7.85   C) 6.93
D) 6.85   E) 7.25

Use the following information and figure for questions 6-7.

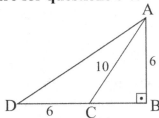

6) **What is the area of triangle ADC?**

A) 42   B) 30   C) 24
D) 18   E) 16

7) **What is the area of triangle ABC?**

A) 48   B) 44   C) 42
D) 24   E) 20

8) **Complete the following statement.**

The area of_____ is side squared.

A) Triangle   B) Square
C) Rectangle   D) Rhombus
E) Trapezoid

Use the following information and figure for questions 9-11.

ABCD is a rectangle, and KLMN is a square.

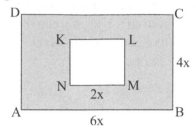

9) What is the ratio of the perimeter of the rectangle and the perimeter of the square?

A) 2 B) 2.5 C) 3
D) 3.5 E) 4

10) What is the ratio of the area of the rectangle and the area of the square?

A) 6 B) 7 C) 8
D) 9 E) 10

11) What is the area of the shaded region?

A) 20x B) 20x^2 C) 10x
D) 10x^2 E) 15x

12) ABCD is a square.

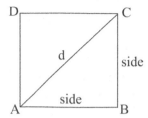

Which is a wrong statement?

A) Area = side x side
B) Perimeter=4 x side
C) Area = $\dfrac{d^2}{2}$
D) Area = side^2
E) All sides are equal

13. The perimeter is 8n–4. What is the area of the square?

A) 4n^2 B) 4n^2–1
C) (2n–1)^2 D) (2n+1)^2
E) 2n^2

14) $\vec{A}=(6, 4x-10)$, $\vec{B}=(2x, 2)$, if $\vec{A} \parallel \vec{B}$, what is the value of x?

A) 1 B) 2 C) 3
D) 4 E) 5

15) $\vec{A}=(8, 4)$, $\vec{B}=(3, 2)$. What is the value of $|\vec{A}-\vec{B}|=$?

A) 20 B) 21 C) 29
D) $\sqrt{29}$ E) 31

TEST 52
(Mixed Geometry Problems)

1) What is the diameter of a circle with circumference 16π?

A) 24   B) 20   C) 18
D) 16   E) 12

2) What is the circumference of a circle with radius 18cm?

A) 48π B) 36π C) 36π
D) 32π E) 16π

3) What is the ratio of the circumference of two circles whose radius is in the ratio 2:7?

A) $\dfrac{2}{7}$ B) $\dfrac{7}{2}$ C) $\dfrac{4}{14}$

D) $\dfrac{14}{4}$ E) $\dfrac{1}{2}$

4) What is the area of the circle with a diameter $4\sqrt{2}$ cm. ?

A) 8π B) 12π C) 16π
D) 12π E) 4π

5) What is the area of the circle with diameter 6x cm?

A) $3x^2\pi$ B) $6x^2\pi$ C) $9x^2\pi$
D) $x^2\pi$ E) $36x^2\pi$

6) What is the length of the arc intercepted by a central of measure 60^0 in a circle with radius is 6cm?

A) 5π B) $\dfrac{5}{\pi}$ C) $\dfrac{\pi}{5}$

D) 6π E) $5\pi^2$

7) What is the diameter of the circle with area 121π cm^2?

A) 32   B) 14   C) 24
D) 22   E) 12

8) What is the radius of the circle with area 169π cm^2?

A) 13   B) 26   C) 13π
D) 6.5   E) 9

9) What is the ratio of the area of the circles with radius in the ratio 4:11?

A) $\dfrac{11}{131}$ B) $\dfrac{4}{13}$ C) $\dfrac{16}{121}$

D) $\dfrac{8}{121}$ E) $\dfrac{3}{11}$

10) What is the difference in the radius of circles with areas 900πcm^2 and 256πcm^2?

A) 14   B) 12   C) 10
D) 8   E) 6

11) **What is the difference in the radius of circles with areas $625\pi cm^2$ and $225\pi cm^2$?**
   A) 10   B) 9   C) 8
   D) 7   E) 6

12) **What is the area of the circle with diameter 8x cm?**
   A) $3x^2\pi$ B) $6x^2\pi$ C) $9x^2\pi$
   D) $16x^2\pi$ E) $36x^2\pi$

13) **Center of the circle is (2, -4) and radius 6cm. What is the equation of the circle?**
   A) $(x-2)^2+(y-4)^2=12$
   B) $(x-2)^2+(y+4)^2=36$
   C) $(x+2)^2+(y+4)^2=18$
   D) $(x-2)^2+(y-4)^2=36$
   E) $(x-2)^2+(y-4)^2=32$

14) **What is the length to the nearest centimeter of diagonal of the square with $15\sqrt{2}$ cm on a side?**
   A) 15   B) 20   C) $20\sqrt{2}$
   D) 30   E) 32

15) **The equilateral triangle has a side length of 20cm. What is the length of the altitude of the triangle?**
   A) 10   B) $10\sqrt{2}$ C) $10\sqrt{3}$
   D) $10\sqrt{5}$ E) 12

TEST 53
(Mixed Geometry Problems)

1) Complete the following statement.

   If two angles of the triangle are congruent to two angles of another triangle, then the triangles are_____.

   A) Right
   B) Complementary
   C) Supplementary
   D) Similar
   E) Different

2) ABC triangle is similar to triangle KLM. AB=10x-8, KL=22cm. What is the value of x?

   A) 3 B) 4 C) 5
   D) 6 E) 8

Use the following information for questions 3-5.

Triangle ABC is similar to triangle KLM. AB=6cm, KL=8cm, BC=9cm, LM=12cm.

3) What is the scale factor of triangles?

   A) $\frac{4}{3}$ B) $\frac{3}{4}$ C) $\frac{9}{14}$
   D) $\frac{9}{15}$ E) $\frac{9}{17}$

4) What is the ratio of the perimeter of triangle ABC and triangle KLM?

   A) $\frac{3}{4}$ B) $\frac{5}{3}$ C) $\frac{4}{5}$
   D) $\frac{5}{4}$ E) $\frac{6}{5}$

5) What is the ratio of the area of triangle ABC and triangle KLM?

   A) $\frac{9}{17}$ B) $\frac{16}{9}$ C) $\frac{9}{16}$
   D) $\frac{10}{9}$ E) $\frac{17}{9}$

6) The ratio of the volume of the cubes is 64:27. What is the ratio of their base area of the cubes?

   A) $\frac{16}{7}$ B) $\frac{16}{10}$ C) $\frac{81}{27}$
   D) $\frac{16}{9}$ E) $\frac{16}{11}$

7) The ratio of the volume of the cubes is 1:8. What is the ratio of their base area of the cubes?

   A) 2 B) 4 C) 1
   D) $\frac{1}{4}$ E) 3

8) The ratio of the area of the circles is 36:25. What is the ratio of their circumference?

A) $\dfrac{3}{4}$ B) $\dfrac{4}{3}$ C) $\dfrac{5}{3}$

D) $\dfrac{6}{5}$ E) $\dfrac{5}{6}$

Use the following information for questions 9-11.

The rectangle ABCD is similar to rectangle KLMN. AD=4, KN=12, DC=5, NM=15cm.

9) What is the scale factor of the rectangle?

A) 4   B) 3   C) $\dfrac{1}{3}$

D) $\dfrac{1}{4}$ E) $\dfrac{1}{5}$

10) What is the ratio of the area of rectangle ABCD and rectangle KLMN?

A) 8   B) 16   C) $\dfrac{1}{9}$

D) $\dfrac{1}{16}$ E) 24

11) What is the ratio of the perimeter of rectangle ABCD and rectangle KLMN?

A) 3   B) $\dfrac{1}{3}$ C) 4

D) $\dfrac{1}{4}$ E) $\dfrac{1}{8}$

12) The ratio of the perimeter of the squares is 7:11. What is the ratio of their side?

A) $\dfrac{11}{7}$ B) $\dfrac{7}{11}$ C) $\dfrac{14}{44}$

D) $\dfrac{49}{121}$ E) $\dfrac{49}{169}$

13) The volume of a rectangular prism is 576cm^3. The base of the prism is 8cm and 6cm. What is the height of the prism?

A) 8cm   B) 10cm   C) 11cm
D) 12cm   E) 16cm

14) The volume of a rectangular prism is 572cm^3. The base of the prism is 5.5cm and 10.4cm. What is the height of the prism?

A) 8cm   B) 10cm   C) 11cm
D) 12cm   E) 16cm

15) $\vec{A} = (3, 8)$, What is the value of $|A|$?

A) 43   B) 63   C) 73
D) $\sqrt{73}$ E) 83

TEST 54
(Mixed Geometry Problems)

1) The perimeter of a square is 3cm. What is the area of the square?

A) $\dfrac{16}{27}$ B) $\dfrac{16}{3}$ C) $\dfrac{81}{27}$

D) $\dfrac{9}{16}$ E) $\dfrac{16}{9}$

2) The perimeter of a square is xcm. What is the area of the square?

A) $\dfrac{x}{16}$ B) $\dfrac{x^2}{16}$ C) $\dfrac{16}{x}$

D) $\dfrac{x^2}{4}$ E) $4x^2$

3) The perimeter of a square is 4k cm. What is the length of the diagonal of the square?

A) $2k$ B) $4k$ C) $k\sqrt{2}$

D) $k^2\sqrt{2}$ E) $2k\sqrt{2}$

4) The length of a diagonal of a square is 6cm. What is the perimeter of the square?

A) $6\sqrt{2}$ B) $2\sqrt{2}$ C) $12\sqrt{2}$

D) $16\sqrt{2}$ E) 24

5) A square area is $81x^2 cm^2$. What is the perimeter of the square?

A) 16x   B) 24x   C) 36x

D) 40x   E) 42x

6) The square area is $\dfrac{9x^2}{4y^2} cm^2$.

What is the perimeter of the square?

A) $\dfrac{6x}{y}$ B) $\dfrac{3x}{y}$ C) $\dfrac{3x}{2y}$

D) $\dfrac{6x}{2y}$ E) $\dfrac{9x}{2y}$

7) The rectangle has edges with lengths of 8cm and 7cm. What is the length of a diagonal of the rectangle?

A) $\sqrt{111}$ B) $\sqrt{113}$ C) $2\sqrt{13}$

D) 14   E) 11.6

Use the following information for questions 8-9.

The lengths of two sides of the rectangle are in the ratio 4:7. The perimeter is 242cm.

8) What is the length of the diagonal of the rectangle?

A) 88.68   B) 124   C) 134.65

D) 144   E) 121

9) What is the area of the rectangle?

A) 3366   B) 3288   C) 3066
D) 3388   E) 3377

10) ABCD is square. K is the midpoint of the diagonal. AK=2x+7, CK=x+14. What is the value of BD?

A) 24   B) 28   C) 32
D) 42   E) 52

Use the following information for questions 11-12.

ABCD is a trapezoid. KL is the mid-segments of trapezoid ABCD. AD= 10cm and BC=20cm.

11) If AB=24 and DC=36, what is the value of KL?

A) 15   B) 20   C) 40
D) 44   E) 52

12) If AK=x+6 and DC=3x+18, what is the value of x?

A) 3   B) 4   C) 5
D) 6   E) 7

13) ABCD is a rectangle. AB=6x–16 and DC=4x+12, what is the value of AB?

A) 48   B) 56   C) 68
D) 72   E) 76

14) ABCD is a rectangle. AC and BD are diagonals. AC=4x–6 and BD=3x+4. What is the value of x?

A) 4   B) 6   C) 8
D) 10   E) 12

15) ABCD is a rhombus. AB=6x–22 and CD=4x+44. What is the value of CD?

A) 176   B) 180   C) 184
D) 190   E) 196

TEST 55
(Mixed Geometry Problems)

1) What is the length of the hypotenuse of the triangle if the lengths of the legs are 8cm and 16cm?

A) 9.56   B) 10   C) 11
D) 12.65   E) 17.89

2) What is the length of the hypotenuse if the lengths of the legs are 10cm and 24cm?

A) 25   B) 26   C) 27
D) 28   E) 32

Use the following information for questions 3-4.

ABC triangle is a right triangle. AC is the hypotenuse. AB=x, BC=x+1, AC=5cm.

3) What is the value of x?
A) 6   B) 7   C) 8
D) 9   E) 12

4) What is the area of triangle ABC?
A) 34cm^2 B) 32cm^2 C) 31cm^2
D) 30cm^2 E) 28cm^2

5) In a right triangle where a and b are the legs and c is the hypotenuse. Which is the triangle?

A) 6, 7, 9   B) 6, 8, 11
C) 5, 12, 14
D) 12, 16, 20
E) 12, 16, 24

6) The perimeter of a square is 24cm. What is the length of a diagonal of the square?

A) 6   B) $6\sqrt{3}$ C) $6\sqrt{2}$
D) 8   E) 9

7) The area of a square is 144cm^2. What is the length of a diagonal of the square?

A) 6   B) 12   C) $12\sqrt{3}$
D) $12\sqrt{2}$ E) $4\sqrt{3}$

8) What is the equation of the line with slope=5, y-intercept =7?

A) y=5x+7   B) y= –7x+5
C) y=7x+5   D) y=5x+9
E) y= –8x–7

9) ∠B=90^0, ∠A=∠C=x. What is the measure of angle BAC?

A) 25
B) 30
C) 35
D) 40
E) 45

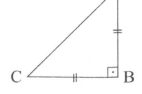

10) What is the area of the parallelogram with base 12 cm and height 10 cm?

A) 30　　B) 60　　C) 120

D) 180　　E) 240

13) What is the volume of the right cylinder with r=5cm and h=6cm?

A) 64π　　B) 64　　C) 100π

D) 100　　E) 150π

11) Each of the interior angles of a regular polygon is 150^0. How many sides does the polygon have?

A) 20　　B) 18　　C) 16

D) 14　　E) 12

14) What is the radius of the circle for $(x–4)^2+(y–5)^2=64$?

A) 8　　B) 9　　C) 10

D) 11　　E) 12

12) What is the circumference of a circle with a radius of 22.5 cm?

A) 45π　　B) 22.5π　　C) 12.5π

D) 11.25π　E) 5π

15) The perimeter of the square is 60 cm. What is the area of the squarc in cm^2?

A) 25　　B) 36　　C) 49

D) 125　　E) 225

Test Answers

Test No	Q1	Q2	Q3	Q4	Q5	Q6	Q7	Q8	Q9	Q10	Q11	Q12	Q13	Q14	Q15
Test 1	A	B	C	A	E	C	B	C	A	D	B	E	C	D	B
Test 2	A	C	D	E	A	D	E	B	C	C	D	E	D	D	E
Test 3	C	A	D	B	E	C	A	D	C	B	D	D	E	A	E
Test 4	E	B	A	D	C	A	A	C	E	D	C	B	C	B	C
Test 5	A	C	B	C	E	D	B	A	E	D	C	E	A	D	B
Test 6	C	B	C	C	A	C	A	B	B	C	C	A	D	B	E
Test 7	A	B	C	E	D	D	B	C	D	C	E	E	A	C	B
Test 8	B	E	D	A	A	C	E	D	A	E	C	B	B	A	B
Test 9	C	A	B	E	E	A	A	E	D	E	C	E	E	D	B
Test 10	E	D	E	D	B	E	D	E	C	A	A	E	B	E	E
Test 11	A	B	A	D	D	D	E	B	C	A	B	E	E	D	D
Test 12	A	A	A	D	E	E	E	E	A	C	D	C	E	E	B
Test 13	E	E	C	E	D	B	E	D	C	E	C	A	E	C	A
Test 14	A	B	E	D	A	D	A	C	C	A	E	E	B	A	D
Test 15	E	E	D	B	C	D	A	A	B	A	A	B	C	D	B
Test 16	B	A	B	C	D	E	B	E	A	C	B	C	E	A	B
Test 17	A	A	A	E	C	A	B	E	B	C	D	B	A	E	B
Test 18	C	A	A	D	C	C	A	E	B	D	E	C	C	E	A
Test 19	A	B	C	C	E	B	D	C	D	E	A	C	A	E	D
Test 20	A	D	C	B	A	B	E	A	E	B	A	C	B	E	D
Test 21	E	E	B	D	E	D	A	A	D	E	A	E	D	E	D
Test 22	C	D	B	E	E	E	B	D	A	C	A	B	B	E	E

Test Answers (Continuous)

Test No	Q1	Q2	Q3	Q4	Q5	Q6	Q7	Q8	Q9	Q10	Q11	Q12	Q13	Q14	Q15
Test 23	B	E	B	C	C	A	E	D	E	E	D	B	A	E	D
Test 24	A	E	E	B	C	A	C	D	B	C	B	D	C	C	A
Test 25	C	D	E	C	A	C	D	A	B	E	E	A	D	C	D
Test 26	D	C	B	B	D	B	E	C	D	A	A	D	C	E	C
Test 27	E	A	E	D	C	C	E	E	E	A	B	D	A	E	E
Test 28	B	E	B	C	B	D	E	B	E	C	C	D	E	E	E
Test 29	A	E	E	D	D	E	D	C	B	D	E	B	D	E	B
Test 30	E	D	B	E	C	B	E	E	C	B	C	B	B	E	A
Test 31	A	B	D	E	E	D	C	B	D	A	D	E	A	A	A
Test 32	E	D	A	B	E	D	A	C	E	D	A	D	B	C	B
Test 33	A	B	D	D	C	E	E	C	A	C	A	D	B	A	B
Test 34	D	B	A	B	A	E	E	B	C	A	B	D	E	B	A
Test 35	B	C	D	E	A	D	C	B	B	B	B	A	C	D	E
Test 36	E	E	B	B	A	E	C	A	A	C	B	D	A	C	B
Test 37	A	B	D	C	A	A	B	C	B	B	A	A	C	A	B
Test 38	A	B	D	A	D	B	A	C	A	B	C	A	D	C	E
Test 39	B	C	A	D	A	A	D	A	E	D	C	B	A	B	C
Test 40	A	C	D	C	A	A	D	D	C	B	A	B	B	D	B
Test 41	D	A	A	C	D	B	B	B	B	A	A	D	D	B	A
Test 42	A	B	C	D	D	A	C	B	D	D	A	C	D	C	C
Test 43	D	A	A	E	E	A	B	B	D	A	B	C	B	C	E
Test 44	A	C	C	A	A	E	B	B	C	D	B	A	A	D	C
Test 45	C	D	B	D	C	A	B	C	C	A	C	D	A	C	C

Test Answers (*Continuous*)

Test No	Q1	Q2	Q3	Q4	Q5	Q6	Q7	Q8	Q9	Q10	Q11	Q12	Q13	Q14	Q15
Test 46	A	A	D	A	D	D	A	D	C	C	D	A	C	A	A
Test 47	B	B	C	A	B	A	B	D	A	B	A	D	C	D	B
Test 48	B	B	D	A	D	A	A	B	C	A	C	D	B	A	D
Test 49	E	D	C	C	C	B	A	C	C	C	D	E	A	A	E
Test 50	B	A	C	D	A	A	C	D	D	C	D	C	D	A	C
Test 51	D	A	B	C	C	D	C	B	B	A	B	C	C	C	D
Test 52	D	C	A	A	C	D	D	A	C	A	A	D	B	A	C
Test 53	D	A	B	A	C	D	D	D	B	C	B	B	D	B	D
Test 54	D	B	C	C	C	A	B	A	D	D	A	D	C	D	A
Test 55	E	B	E	D	D	C	D	A	E	C	E	A	E	A	E

The Authors

Tayyip Oral, MBA

Tayyip Oral is a mathematician and test prep expert who has been teaching in learning centers and high school test since 1998. Mr. Oral is the founder of 555 math book series which includes a variety of mathematics books. Tayyip Oral graduated from Qafqaz university with a Bachelor`s degree in Industrial Engineering. He later received his Master`s degree in Business Administration from the same university. He is an educator who has written several SAT Math, ACT Math, Geometry, Math counts, and Math IQ books. He lives in Houston, TX.

Veysel Karatas, M. Ed.

Veysel Karatas graduated with Bachelor's degree in technical teacher education with teaching certification at Suleyman Demirel University to become a carrier and technical education teacher in high schools in 2003. He worked in public schools as a mathematics teacher for six years in Texas. He is a certified Mathematics teacher in grades 4-12. He has experience in teaching Mathematics in middle and high school and coaching Mathcounts team for middle school students. He completed Master of Education in Curriculum Instruction in Mathematics Education at North American University in May 2017. He is currently studying in the Doctor of Education in Curriculum and Instruction in Mathematics Education at the University of Texas Rio Grande Valley.

Books by Tayyip Oral

1. Tayyip Oral, Dr. Steve Warner. 555 Math IQ Questions for Middle School Students: Improve Your Critical Thinking with 555 Questions and Answer, 2015

2. Tayyip Oral, Dr. Steve Warner, Serife Oral, Algebra Handbook for Gifted Middle School Students, 2015

3. Tayyip Oral, Geometry Formula Handbook, 2015

4. Tayyip Oral, IQ Intelligence Questions for Middle and High School Students, 2014

5. Tayyip Oral, Dr. Steve Warner, Serife Oral, 555 Geometry Problems for High School Students: 135 Questions with Solutions, 2015

6. Tayyip Oral, Sevket Oral, 555 Math IQ questions for Elementary School Student, 2015

7. Tayyip Oral, 555 ACT Math, 555 Questions with Solutions, 2015

8. Tayyip Oral, Sevket Oral, 555 ACT Math - II, 555 Questions with Answers, 2016

9. Tayyip Oral, 555 Geometry (555 Questions with Solutions), 2016

10. Tayyip Oral, Dr. Steve Warner, 555 Advanced math problems, 2015

11. T. Oral, E. Seyidzade, Araz publishing, Master's Degree Program Preparation (IQ), Cag Ogretim, Araz Courses, Baku, Azerbaijan, 2010.
    A master's degree program preparation textbook for undergraduate students in Azerbaijan.

12. T. Oral, M. Aranli, F. Sadigov, and N. Resullu, Resullu Publishing, Baku, Azerbaijan - 2012 (3.edition)
    A textbook for job placement exam in Azerbaijan for undergraduate and post-undergraduate students in Azerbaijan.

13. T. Oral and I. Hesenov, Algebra (Textbook), Nurlar Printing and Publishing, Baku, Azerbaijan, 2001.
    A textbook covering algebra concepts and questions with detailed explanations at high school level in Azerbaijan.

14. T.Oral, I.Hesenov, S.Maharramov, and J.Mikaylov, Geometry (Textbook), Nurlar Printing and Publishing, Baku, Azerbaijan, 2002.
    A textbook for high school students to prepare them for undergraduate education in Azerbaijan.

15. T. Oral, I. Hesenov, and S. Maharramov, Geometry Formulas (Text Book), Araz courses, Baku, Azerbaijan, 2003.
    A textbook for high school students' university exam preparation in Azerbaijan.

16. T. Oral, I. Hesenov, and S. Maharramov, Algebra Formulas (Text Book), Araz courses, Baku, Azerbaijan, 2000
    A university exam preparation textbook for high school students in Azerbaijan.